Steam in the Scottish Landscape

MICHAEL WELCH

Capital Transport

ISBN 978-1-85414-332-7

Published by
Capital Transport Publishing
www.capitaltransport.com

Printed by
1010 Printing International

Front cover: A shot of the tiny station at Killin on 14th April 1961 with a former Caledonian Railway 0-4-4T, No.55217, waiting to leave with a train to Killin Junction on the Callander to Crianlarich Lower line. Passenger trains originally ran to Loch Tay, a mile beyond here, but these ceased in 1939. The locomotive shed was located at Loch Tay, however, so the line remained in use purely for access purposes to the shed. Regrettably, this branch, which was surrounded by some of the most magnificent scenery imaginable, was officially closed to all traffic from 1st November 1965. *Colour-Rail*

Back Cover: The snowy wastes of Gleneagles! Fresh snow carpets the platforms as a three-coach Edinburgh Princes Street–Perth train steams off into the distance behind BR Standard Class 4MT 2-6-4T No.80093 on 20th February 1964. Besides being one of the most beautifully situated stations on the Glasgow to Aberdeen line, Gleneagles was also the junction for the Crieff and Comrie branch which diverged on the left of the picture. Branch trains normally used the loop platform on the left, but there were connections with the main line both north and south of the station: part of the layout at the north end is visible. The branch lost its passenger service from 6th July 1964. *Ken Falconer*

Title page: A charming scene, showing a nicely cleaned former Caledonian Railway 0-4-4T No.55218 at Aberfeldy, after arrival from Ballinluig with a two-coach train on 13th September 1958. Note the ancient scales on the platform and the hanging flower basket. This locomotive was officially allocated to Perth shed at the time, but no doubt spent long periods away from its home depot working from the small sub-shed at Aberfeldy. *Gerald Daniels*

Introduction

Glenfinnan viaduct, Beattock summit, Rannoch Moor and the Forth bridge are immediately recognisable as landmarks on the Scottish railway system. The relatively low population density north of the border did not justify the dense network of lines, except in the central lowland belt, that can be found in other parts of Great Britain but what Scotland may have lacked in route mileage was more than compensated for by the breathtaking scenery through which the lines were constructed. In steam days a wonderful assortment of locomotive classes could be found in Scotland, ranging from diminutive former Highland Railway 0-4-4Ts on the Dornoch branch to mighty 'Princess Coronation' Pacifics on the heaviest West Coast Main Line expresses. Some parts of Scotland have high annual rainfall, as many visitors have experienced, but when the rain clears and the mist lifts a landscape of unparalleled natural beauty is revealed.

Many of the lines in Scotland are characterised by heavy gradients and one of the best known, and certainly the most heavily trafficked, is the climb over Beattock summit on the West Coast Main Line between Carlisle and Glasgow. The approach from the north, along the valley of the river Clyde, is gradual with fairly moderate grades, but northbound trains face an arduous climb, mostly at 1 in 75 or thereabouts, from Beattock station to the summit and the heavier trains were always banked. The sight and sound of a heavy express hauled by a 'Princess Coronation' Pacific ascending the incline with a 'banker' pushing for all it was worth at the rear was not easily forgotten. The other steeply graded Anglo-Scottish line was the much lamented Waverley route from Carlisle to Edinburgh, the section south of Hawick having featured climbs in each direction across bare moorland up to an isolated signal box at Whitrope summit. Riccarton, where there was a small railway community, was formerly the junction station for the line to Hexham and probably one of the most inaccessible on the BR network, served only by tracks across the moorland. Fortunately, the distinctive sound of Gresley-designed V2 Class 2-6-2s doing battle with the line's tortuous 1 in 75 grades has been captured for posterity on disc thanks to the efforts of the late Peter Handford. Inclines on the former Glasgow & South Western line from Carlisle to Glasgow via Dumfries were tame in comparison, but compensation was provided by the scenic Drumlanrig gorge, between Dumfries and Kirkconnel.

Scotland's most scenic routes are those north of the central lowland industrial belt and in the twilight years of steam the Glasgow to Aberdeen became one of the last lines in Great Britain where express passenger trains were regularly rostered for steam haulage and attracted enthusiasts from far and wide. This stemmed from a decision taken in 1962 to use steam power on the accelerated service in preference to under-powered diesel locomotives not noted for their reliability. A trial run took place in February 1962 and the improved service commenced on 18th June. A small pool of Gresley's legendary Class A4 Pacifics, supplemented by other classes, was allocated for use on the route and surplus engines in good condition south of the border were stored in reserve. This policy was in complete contrast to the trend of increasing dieselisation in other areas. Some sections of the route had long, level straight stretches where the Pacifics could show their mettle and it is no wonder that many steam enthusiasts made the pilgrimage to Scotland to experience an exhilarating run or photograph the magnificent A4s. The end came for steam on the line in September 1966 when the Scottish Region ran a commemorative special. This route may not have had the scenic splendours of others but will unquestionably best be remembered among steam enthusiasts as the final stamping ground of the illustrious Class A4 Pacifics.

Unlike the Aberdeen line, the Glasgow to Inverness route was an early candidate for dieselisation and, alas, does not appear to have been widely photographed in colour in steam days. It diverged from the former route at Stanley Junction, seven miles north of Perth, and follows the meandering river Tay for a while before threading Glen Garry and surmounting Druimuachdar summit (1,484 feet above sea level), the highest point on the British main line railway network. There are substantial climbs in each direction to the summit, and after leaving Blair Athol northbound trains face fifteen miles of tough climbing, mostly at 1 in 70 or thereabouts. The gradients in the opposite direction are not quite as daunting, but even so involve sections of 1 in 80. Between Aviemore and Inverness lies Slochd summit (1,315 feet) which is approached on 1 in 60 gradients in each direction. Needless to say, the scenery along the entire line is absolutely breathtaking with magnificent views of tumbling rivers, lochs and mountain peaks.

Perhaps the most famous route of all in Scotland is the West Highland, from Glasgow to Fort William, which offers unrivalled, panoramic vistas not obtainable from any road. The line, which was built cheaply and generally follows the lie of the land where possible, is noteworthy for a series of summits, the first being at Glen Douglas, north of Garelochhead. After passing through Crianlarich trains pass over County March summit before negotiating the remarkable Horseshoe curve, between Tyndrum and Bridge of Orchy, with Ben Dorain (3,524 feet) towering above the single track which is almost lost in the landscape. Later the West Highland line crosses Rannoch Moor, a bleak and inhospitable wilderness, before reaching the highest point of the line at lonely Corrour station which can only be reached by rough mountain tracks. From Corrour, amidst absolutely stunning scenery, the line descends at 1 in 67 to Tulloch, running on a ledge above remote Loch Treig for mile after mile. The Tulloch to Fort William section does not quite match the scenic wonders of other parts of the route, the highlight being passage of Monessie gorge. Fort William is the starting point for the Mallaig Extension that has splendid delights all of its own, most notably Glenfinnan viaduct, unbeatable views from the viaduct at the head of Loch Nan Uamh and lovely vistas from Arisaig of the inner Hebridean islands of Rhum and Eigg.

North of Inverness the route to the Kyle of Lochalsh is simply outstanding, especially the passage of Glen Carron and the western end of the line where it winds around Loch Carron and plunges through each successive hillock in a vertical-sided rock cutting. Achnasheen is the busiest station on the route from where road transport gives access to Loch Maree, Glen Torridon and Gairloch. The route has some very steep gradients, especially the taxing climb from Achnashellach to the summit at Luib which is 646 feet above sea level.

The line to Wick and Thurso does not quite have the drama of other lines, but the short branch from The Mound to the small cathedral city of Dornoch was a real gem. The workings on this line, which often ran as mixed trains, were latterly powered by GWR-designed pannier tank locomotives that replaced the Highland Railway 0-4-4Ts previously used.

I would like to record my appreciation to all those photographers who kindly made their precious transparencies available for publication in this album, thus reaching a much wider audience. In addition, John Beckett, Chris Evans, David Fakes, John Langford and Roger Merry-Price have read through the text and suggested many corrections and improvements. Design and typesetting by Lucy Frontani. I accept responsibility for any mistakes that have remained undetected.

Michael Welch
Burgess Hill,
West Sussex,
May 2009

Contents

A peep inside Edinburgh Princes Street, the Caledonian Railway's (CR) principal station in the city, showing Stanier Class 5MT No.45011 awaiting departure with the 1.20pm train to Glasgow Central on 31st July 1965. The first CR station in Edinburgh was their Lothian Road terminus which opened on 15th February 1848. In 1870 a 'temporary' terminus was opened in Princes Street but this was destroyed by fire on 16th June 1890. This event prompted the CR to construct a new, much grander station and this opened in stages between 1890 and 1893; it had seven platforms and an 850 feet-long roof. A hotel was added ten years later. After the Second World War the number of trains using Princes Street station declined, the service to Balerno being axed from 13th June 1949 while the last train to Leith North ran on 30th April 1962. When the local services to Carstairs ended in 1964 the writing was really on the wall for Princes Street station and all of its remaining trains were diverted to Waverley station from 6th September 1965, the last trains running on 4th September. The final services were the 10.30pm SO to Lanark, with Class 5MT No.45171 in charge, while the 11.30pm to Birmingham was hauled by sister engine No.44954. *Ken Falconer*

The 5.20pm to Glasgow Central waits to leave Princes Street station on 31st August 1964. The locomotive in charge is Stanier Class 5MT 4-6-0 No.45155 which, at the time of this photograph, was based at Dalry Road shed. This shed was located close to Princes Street station and provided motive power for many services that originated from the station. *Ken Falconer*

The first railway in Edinburgh was the Edinburgh & Dalkeith, opened in 1831, a horse-drawn line built to link the city with a nearby coalfield. The first major route was the Edinburgh & Glasgow Railway, opened in 1842 while in 1846 the line southwards to Berwick-upon-Tweed was brought into use. In 1890 the opening of the Forth Bridge brought a further increase in traffic to the already congested lines through Waverley station and the North British Railway (NBR) proposed the quadrupling of the route through Princes Street Gardens, which are so beloved by the people of Edinburgh. This proposal caused immediate uproar but, even so, the work was authorised by an Act of 5th July 1891 and a strip of the gardens was sacrificed in the name of progress. Here, Class A1 Pacific No.60124 *Kenilworth,* in commendably clean condition, is seen passing the attractive gardens with an unidentified relief train on 22nd June 1965. A total of fifty of these handsome locomotives was built, in 1948/49, but the class was tragically short-lived with withdrawals commencing in 1962 as diesels replaced them. *Kenilworth* was the penultimate survivor, not being withdrawn until March 1966. *Ken Falconer*

The 22nd of March 1963 seems to have been a particularly gloomy and overcast day in Edinburgh, but the spirits of steam enthusiasts visiting Waverley station were surely lifted by the splendid sight of 'Princess Coronation' Pacific No.46257 *City of Salford* waiting to leave at the head of the 10.00am train to Inverness. No.46257 would presumably have hauled the train as far as Perth where diesel traction would have taken over. One wonders what was going through the driver's mind as he awaited the 'right away'. He certainly could not have been wishing for a larger and more powerful engine! Note the barrow loaded with mailbags, and corridor connection shield lying on the platform at the base of the lamp standard. *Ken Falconer*

The 1.18pm Edinburgh to Crail, on the long-closed Fife coast line, pulls out of Waverley station on 25th August 1962. The reconstruction of the station, and its approach lines, took place between 1892 and 1900 and this involved considerable civil engineering works. New tunnels were cut between Haymarket and Princes Street Gardens on the western side and through Calton Hill on the eastern side. The station itself was built on a central island, covered 23 acres and its nineteen platforms were said to have an aggregate length of 13,980ft. The vast bulk of the North British hotel dominates the picture on the left, while passengers riding on the top deck of those colourful, vintage Edinburgh Corporation buses have an excellent view of Class B1 4-6-0 No.61147 making its departure. *Ken Falconer*

Nothing stirs the imagination quite as much as a steam railway at night. The crimson glow from the fire 'dancing' on the billowing exhaust, sparks from the locomotive's chimney and rhythmic clanking of the motion as an engine passes by, largely unseen, in the darkness. In this illustration Stanier Class 5MT No.44700 simmers at the buffer stops in Edinburgh Waverley station after arrival with the 4.35pm from Liverpool on 28th April 1964. *Ken Falconer*

An unidentified down passenger train passes Longniddry on 11th August 1962 behind Class A1 Pacific No.60155 *Borderer,* which was one of a small number of this class fitted with roller bearings. When the line from Edinburgh to Berwick-upon-Tweed was proposed the directors of the NBR toyed with the idea of routing the line through the nearby town of Haddington, where several wealthy and influential people lived, but engineers advised against this plan due to the high costs involved. It was subsequently decided to build a branch from Longniddry to Haddington and this opened on 22nd June 1846, the same day that services commenced between the Scottish capital and Berwick. The branch proved to be unremunerative, however, and was closed from 5th December 1949. *Ken Falconer*

The 3.30pm Edinburgh to Berwick-upon-Tweed stopping train, formed of three non-gangway suburban coaches, was certainly well provided with motive power on 7th May 1962. It was photographed after leaving Penmanshiel tunnel with Class A2/3 Pacific No.60521 *Watling Street* in charge. The tunnel, located between the former Cockburnspath and Grantshouse stations, hit the headlines when a partial collapse occurred during reconstruction on 17th March 1979, regrettably claiming the lives of two workers whose bodies were never recovered. A new route was built avoiding the tunnel and the Penmanshiel diversion line opened on 20th August 1979. *Ken Falconer*

EAST COAST MAIN LINE

An up local pick-up freight working, hauled by B1 Class 4-6-0 No.61076, passes Reston on 31st May 1963. The majority of the 410 engines in this class were constructed by the North British Locomotive Company, while other large batches were built at Darlington, Gorton (Manchester) and Vulcan Foundry. The machine depicted here was a North British product and outshopped in September 1946: it remained in service until September 1965. The photographer comments that No.61076 appeared later in the day hauling the 3.45pm Dunbar to Edinburgh passenger train tender-first, so it had presumably only worked the freight as far as Berwick-upon-Tweed or Tweedmouth before retracing its steps back to Dunbar. Reston station, the erstwhile junction for the branch to Duns, was closed from 4th May 1964. *John Langford*

The directors of the NBR were firm in their belief that a branch from Reston to Duns would generate new traffic and the 8¾ miles-long line was opened on 15th August 1849. The directors' optimism was such that it was built as a double track route, but traffic was way below expectations and the line was reduced to a single track as early as 1857. The Berwickshire Railway was formed to build a line from Duns to Ravenswood Junction, on the Edinburgh to Carlisle Waverley route, just north of St Boswells. It seems that the over-optimistic promoters had in mind a cross-country line providing a direct link between the East Coast Main Line and the Waverley route, but their route duplicated the Berwick-upon-Tweed–Kelso–St Boswells line and served no substantial intermediate settlements. Despite these disadvantages it was opened to traffic in stages and trains started running throughout on 2nd October 1865. The Reston–Duns–St Boswells line then led a quiet existence until it was severed by flooding between Duns and Earlston on 13th August 1948, a blow from which it never recovered. Passenger trains ceased to run between Duns and St Boswells, although freight trains were later reinstated over part of the line. The 1951 summer timetable advertised only four trains each way over the eastern end of the route, from Reston to Duns, and these were withdrawn from 10th September 1951. Here, Ivatt Class 2MT 2-6-0 No.46475 poses in the sunshine at Duns on 31st May 1963 after working the branch freight from Reston. *John Langford*

When the late Doctor (later Lord) Beeching became chairman of the British Transport Commission he quickly identified that much of BR's freight operation was totally uneconomic and was ripe for drastic rationalisation. He certainly would not have approved of the type of operation seen in this picture which shows a group of men unloading (what appear to be) bags of animal feed or, perhaps, fertilizer from a wagon in the goods yard at Duns on 31st May 1963. This sort of operation tied up wagons for days on end during which time they were not earning their keep. Another wagon, doubtless containing coal for the local merchant, is on the left of the shot. One wonders how long that would have been sitting in the yard. A way of life that was shortly to be consigned to the history books! Freight services along the remnant of the Reston to Duns branch ceased on 7th November 1966. *John Langford*

Generations of railway photographers have complained about promising pictures being ruined at the last minute by the sun disappearing behind a cloud and suchlike, but on this occasion the photographer had luck on his side – just for a change! This picture shows NBR Class J37 0-6-0 No.64591 at remote Greenlaw with the 7.30am freight from St Boswells on 31st May 1963. This was the remaining stub of the St Boswells to Duns line that was washed away by floods in 1948, as previously stated. By the date of this picture the freight was booked to be worked by a 350hp diesel shunter based at Galashiels, but both the local shunters were stopped for exams and this Class J37 had to be commandeered from St Margarets shed, Edinburgh, to work the train. *John Langford*

The tweed towns in the borders region suffered from a lack of adequate transport links, and power to work the mills, so the North British Railway vowed to connect every one with the Lothian coalfield. The Edinburgh & Hawick Railway was authorised on 31st July 1845 and opened on 1st November 1849. It linked the two main towns, Hawick and Galashiels, with Edinburgh and various extensions were built to other towns in the area. The NBR saw Carlisle as its ultimate goal, however, but Hawick and Carlisle were separated by miles of barren moorland with little prospect of originating traffic. The rival Caledonian Railway was interested in building a line from Carlisle and the NBR wished to retain their territorial advantage in the area. The result was the Border Union Railway Act of 21st July 1859 and the line, together with some small branches, opened on 1st July 1862. It was known as the Waverley route, the title being inspired by the novels of Sir Walter Scott. In this picture B1 Class 4-6-0 No.61350 is seen between Tynehead and Falahill with the 4.10pm Edinburgh Waverley to Hawick train on 26th July 1963. The long climb up to Falahill, much of it at 1 in 70 or thereabouts, was the first obstacle facing crews of southbound trains after leaving Edinburgh but in this shot No.61350 is 'blowing off' and appears to have been untroubled by its effort to reach the summit. *Ken Falconer*

A Stephenson Locomotive Society/Branch Line Society rail tour from Edinburgh, with Gresley A4 Class Pacific No.60031 *Golden Plover* in charge, waits to leave Galashiels on 18th April 1965. Galashiels, 33½ miles from Edinburgh Waverley, was one of the principal stations on the Waverley route, but in the summer 1964 timetable it was provided with a rather meagre service of just eight trains each way on weekdays which reflected the very low traffic potential of the area. Some of the wayside stations between Edinburgh and Galashiels only had a token service of just one or two trains a day, and for some the last northbound train on Mondays to Fridays was the 8.02am from Hawick which arrived in Edinburgh at 9.46am! There was, however, a later service on Saturdays which reached Edinburgh at 1.49pm. *Roy Hobbs*

Photographed on a wretchedly gloomy day, V2 Class 2-6-2 No.60931 exerts maximum effort as it struggles to keep the 8.16am Millerhill to Carlisle freight on the move. Could the photographer have wished for a more spectacular smoke effect? This picture was taken south of Hawick on 23rd April 1965. This locomotive was constructed at Doncaster Works in September 1941 and remained in service until September 1965. *John Beckett*

Shankend viaduct is one of the Waverley route's outstanding civil engineering structures and in this picture No.60931 is seen crossing the viaduct with the train seen in the previous shot. The Class V2 is doing battle with the fierce gradient, much of it at 1 in 75, that applies all of the way from Hawick to the summit just beyond Whitrope tunnel. One can only imagine the wonderful exhaust noise being emitted by the V2 as it charged across the viaduct, shattering the peace of this quiet, remote location. These locomotives had a very distinctive staccato-like exhaust beat and the sound of them at work on the Waverley route was immortalised on disc by the late Peter Handford. He was not averse to recording at night-time when there was no other noise to be heard out on the desolate moors apart from the distant hooting of an owl. *John Beckett*

It is No.60931 again! Here it heads away from Whitrope tunnel with the 8.16am Millerhill to Carlisle freight on the same day as the previous shots were taken. This spot was a summit in both directions and the crew of No.60931 were no doubt relieved that the rest of the journey to Carlisle would be much easier for them after negotiating around twelve miles of unrelenting grades, mostly at 1 in 75/80, from Hawick. Freight workings over the Waverley route were officially partly dieselised from 7th May 1962 but in practice steam continued to appear regularly for almost another four years, no doubt as a result of the unreliability of the diesel fleet. One of the most spectacular workings was a heavy Halewood to Bathgate car train which was double-headed over the route, and on 12th June 1964 the return empty train produced two 'Britannia' Pacifics! The closing years of steam traction were a fascinating mix of Edinburgh-based Class A3s, A4s, V2s and B1s interspersed with 'Britannia' Pacifics and Stanier Class 5MTs working from the Carlisle end of the line. On at least one occasion a 'Black Five' piloted a V2 on a loaded car train – what an amazing combination! *John Beckett*

The inhospitable, bleak and bare moorland through which the Hawick to Carlisle section of the Waverley route passed is exemplified in this picture taken near Riccarton Junction on 23rd April 1966. The train depicted is a Manchester to Edinburgh rail tour with Class A2 Pacific No.60528 *Tudor Minstrel* in charge, and no doubt the locomotive made a memorable sound as it climbed the 1 in 75 gradient that applies at this point. Apparently, A4 Class Pacific No.60024 *Kingfisher* had been rostered to work the train from Carlisle to Edinburgh, but had been ruled out due to it having a leaky valve and being rather 'off beat'. When this section of the route was being built there were misgivings among some NBR directors who doubted the line's financial viability. The route's fortunes improved, however, when the Midland Railway reached Carlisle in 1876 but, even so, receipts on the Hawick to Carlisle section remained abysmal, and to make matters worse it was a very expensive line to operate due to its isolation and vulnerability to snow blockages in the wintertime. *Charles Whetmath*

The river Esk is in the background as a rather grubby Class A4 Pacific No.60027 *Merlin* heads northwards near Longtown on 5th June 1965 with what was supposedly an A3 Class commemorative rail tour from Edinburgh to Carlisle and back, outwards via Newcastle, the return journey being along the Waverley route. Unfortunately No.60052 *Prince Palatine* had succumbed with a hot axlebox at Carlisle but participants were no doubt quite happy when Kingmoor shed provided *Merlin* as a suitable replacement. This machine was one of two A4 Pacifics, the other being No.60031 *Golden Plover,* disfigured by a diagonal yellow stripe on the cab side indicating that the locomotive concerned was prohibited under the wires south of Crewe! *John Beckett*

Stanier Class 5MT No.44900 lays a considerable smokescreen across the tracks north of Beattock station as it starts the ascent to the summit on 24th August 1961. The Class 5MT is hauling only a fairly modest load and does not appear to be taking the assistance of a banking engine – certainly there is no 'banker' waiting in the yard on the right of the picture. The line from Carlisle to Glasgow and Edinburgh was authorised on 31st July 1845 and opened throughout by the Caledonian Railway (CR) on the 15th February 1848. It was extended to link up with the Scottish Central Railway at Castlecary, this being achieved in August 1848. The CR waited for the main line to 'consolidate' before regular traffic commenced, one of the first through workings from London apparently being a mail train that the Post Office had transferred from the East Coast route. The first passenger-carrying express from the capital to Glasgow/Edinburgh operated on 1st May 1848. *Martin Smith*

Stanier Class 5MT 4-6-0 No.44675 'blows off' as it comes cautiously down the bank towards Beattock station with an up freight on the same day as the previous photograph. Rather unusually, the train has some passenger coaches in its consist which were probably *en route* to works for overhaul. The line veering off on the right at a lower level is the somewhat obscure branch to the little spa town of Moffat. This was promoted locally in order to provide easy access for the masses and opened on 2nd April 1883. The passenger service survived until 6th December 1954, while goods trains continued until 6th April 1964. *Martin Smith*

The majesty of steam. One of the most thrilling and unforgettable sights (not to mention sounds!) during the last years of Scottish steam was that of a heavy train ascending Beattock bank with locomotives at each end. In this picture Stanier 'Princess Coronation' Class 8P Pacific No.46223 *Princess Alice,* assisted at the rear by an unknown 2-6-4T engine, heaves a massive fourteen-coach overnight London to Glasgow express up the 1 in 74 gradient near Greskine on 5th September 1959. What finer spectacle could there be? The Stanier Pacifics were immensely powerful, but not even one of these magnificent machines could tackle the long, steep and unrelenting climb up to Beattock summit with such a load unassisted.
Colour-Rail

The 12.10am Euston to Glasgow sleeping car train is given vigorous rear-end assistance by BR Standard 2-6-4T No.80002 on the unrelenting climb to Beattock summit on 27th July 1963. An especially interesting aspect of operations on Beattock bank was a regular Saturdays only passenger working run solely for railway staff and their families who lived at various lineside cottages between Beattock station and the summit. It was known as the 'Siege', apparently because it was introduced at about the time of Mafeking (1899/1900). The one-coach train left the summit at 10.20am and returned from Beattock station at 12.20pm, passengers boarding/alighting by means of a ladder carried in the guard's compartment. There was even a Saturday evening train that ran as required from Beattock station. Sadly, this unique working has long since been abandoned and become a part of railway folklore – one wonders if it was ever used by railway photographers endeavouring to reach remote locations.
Martin Smith

Drama on Beattock bank! Things did not always go according to plan on Beattock bank, even when an assisting locomotive was taken, and in this view a northbound freight is seen restarting after stalling on the bank. At first sight the train may not appear to be a particularly long one, but this can be deceptive because the wagons could contain a heavy mineral and the train may actually weigh much more than one would think. The train engine is Stanier Class 5MT No.44969 and the 'banker' is Fairburn-designed 4MT Class 2-6-4T No.42693, which was allocated to Beattock shed primarily for banking duties. The Class 5MT may not have been in the best of condition as it was withdrawn in December 1963, a little over five months after this shot was taken on 27th July. *Martin Smith*

A scene at Abington, one of the small wayside stations between Carlisle and Carstairs, showing a very grimy BR Standard 6P5F Class Pacific No.72006 *Clan Mackenzie* pausing with a Carlisle to Glasgow Central stopping train, on 27th July 1963. By the date of this photograph all of the Scottish Region-based members of this class had been withdrawn but the LMR Carlisle Kingmoor-allocated engines continued to work across the border into Scotland, as seen here. Apart from Beattock and Lockerbie, both of which had a reasonable service, all of the intermediate stations between Carlisle and Carstairs had a very meagre service indeed, the summer 1963 timetable advertising only two morning trains to Glasgow and two return workings. *Ken Falconer*

In total contrast to the filthy 'Clan' Pacific seen in the previous shot, here an immaculately turned-out member of the class, No.72009 *Clan Stewart*, is seen leaving Carstairs with the 9.25am Crewe to Aberdeen train on 1st August 1964. Note the fine signal gantry on the left of the picture. This train would have been routed via Coatbridge (Central), Stirling, Perth and Forfar and was booked to arrive in the 'Granite City' at 7.38pm. Built at Crewe and outshopped in April 1952, No.72009 was destined to have a pathetically short working life, lasting in service until August 1965. *Ken Falconer*

The dying days of the famous 'Royal Scot' class. In this portrait Stanier Class 7P 4-6-0 No.46115 *Scots Guardsman* makes a smoky exit from Carstairs with the 1.12pm relief train from Liverpool to Glasgow on 31st July 1965. There were originally 71 engines in this class but during the first half of the 1960s their ranks were steadily depleted by withdrawals and by the beginning of 1965 a mere five examples remained in traffic. By the date of this picture only Nos.46115 and 46140 survived, the latter being withdrawn in November whilst No.46115 lasted a further month, thus becoming the final member of the class in service, based at Carlisle Kingmoor shed. On 31st December 1965 *Scots Guardsman* was specially cleaned and rostered to work the 1.32pm Carlisle to Perth train (9.25am from Crewe) as a farewell tribute to the class and by all accounts put in a competent performance. On 3rd January 1966 No.46115 was noted dead in the yard at Kingmoor shed following its withdrawal from traffic but it subsequently had the good fortune to survive into preservation. *Ken Falconer*

Another picture taken at Carstairs, this time showing Stanier 'Princess Royal' Class 8P Pacific No.46203 *Princess Margaret Rose* leaving with the 10.00am London Euston to Perth train on 18th August 1962. When passenger services on the West Coast Main Line were being dieselised the entire complement of 'Princess Royal' Pacifics was identified as being 'surplus to requirements' and put into store in early 1961 at various locations, and in some cases the nameplates were removed for safe keeping. Locomotives were stored at Willesden, Rugby, Carlisle Kingmoor and, rather strangely, Carnforth. No.46203 was stored at the last-mentioned shed together with No.46211 *Queen Maud*. In June 1961 some of the class were returned to service, including *Princess Margaret Rose,* but others were not so fortunate and remained out of traffic. Six engines were withdrawn in the autumn of that year whilst the remainder, including No.46203, returned to store. In January 1962 there was a motive power shortage and, predictably, the services of the 'Princess Royals' were needed once again and they were all returned to service. The survivors stayed in traffic until they were all withdrawn in the autumn and this celebrated class was no more. *Ken Falconer*

An evening suburban train leaves Glasgow Central in September 1960. Motive power is provided by Fairburn-designed 4MT Class 2-6-4T No.42689 which was built at Derby works in August 1945 and lasted in traffic until October 1967. Locomotives of this class were a very common sight at this station prior to electrification of the suburban lines and at the time of this picture Glasgow Polmadie and Motherwell sheds shared an allocation of around thirty engines. *Colour-Rail*

The 'Royal Scot', with gleaming 'Princess Coronation' Class 8P Pacific No.46223 *Princess Alice* in charge, awaits departure from Glasgow Central on 28th May 1959. This prestigious service was one of the crack trains of the day on the West Coast Main Line and in the winter 1959/60 timetable was advertised to leave Glasgow at 10.00am with an arrival time in London Euston of 5.15pm. On some Sundays the 'Royal Scot' was scheduled to run to and from Buchanan Street station and ran to a much slower schedule due to engineering works. Surprisingly, perhaps, the down train was booked to stop at Beattock, a station that was subsequently closed. The train's title can be traced back to 1927 and it is a remarkable fact that after the Second World War it frequently comprised no fewer that seventeen coaches, a mammoth formation by any standard. In November 1959 the 'Royal Scot' became a strictly limited train with reserved seats throughout its eight-coach formation. *R. C. Riley*

Photographed on a dreary day, Rebuilt 'Patriot' Class 7P 4-6-0 No.45530 *Sir Frank Ree* is depicted on the long descent towards Dumfries with a Glasgow to Carlisle goods train on 11th June 1965. By the time of this picture only two of these locomotives remained in traffic, the other one being No.45531 *Sir Frederick Harrison,* and No.45530 gained the dubious distinction of being the last example in service, being taken out of traffic in December 1965. It had been disfigured by a diagonal yellow stripe on the cab side, which is just visible, indicating that it was not permitted to work south of Crewe due to the danger of members of the crew touching the overhead line. *John Beckett*

The Carlisle to Glasgow via Dumfries line was largely promoted by two companies. The Glasgow Paisley Kilmarnock & Ayr Railway (GPK&AR) proposed an extension southwards from Kilmarnock, which had been reached from Glasgow via Dalry on 4th April 1843, while the Glasgow Dumfries & Carlisle Railway (GD&CR) aimed to build a line northwards to meet the GPK&AR near Old Cumnock. In the event Parliament decreed that the Dumfries Company must share the Caledonian Railway's tracks from Gretna, but apart from that amendment both companies' bills were successful. The route was opened in stages and trains started running between Kilmarnock and Auchinleck on 9th August 1848, while at the southern end of the line services commenced from Dumfries to Gretna later the same month. The entire route was opened throughout on 28th October 1850 when the aforementioned companies amalgamated to form the Glasgow & South Western Railway. The Kilmarnock to Glasgow via Stewarton route opened throughout in 1873. The line is moderately graded, one of the longest climbs being the steady seventeen miles-long ascent, mostly at 1 in 150/200, from Dumfries to Drumlanrig tunnel. In this picture Stanier Class 5MT 4-6-0 No.45124 is seen battling uphill near Closeburn with a northbound freight on 22nd April 1965. *John Beckett*

Signs in light blue, the ScR's regional colour, chalked notices and a fingerboard indicating that the next departure was for Irvine and Ardrossan. This was the delightful scene at Platform One on Kilmarnock station on 3rd June 1963. There was, apparently, an office dealing solely with telegrams! The local train service between Kilmarnock and Ardrossan via Irvine, which was rather irregular, was withdrawn from 6th April 1964 so the fingerboard would have been declared redundant within a year of this shot being taken. *John Langford*

Hauling the two-coach 11.56am SO Glasgow St Enoch to Kilmarnock stopping train is unlikely to have unduly extended 'Black Five' No.45007 which was photographed after arrival at its destination on 13th April 1963. One wonders whether the fares covered the cost of the coal! At the time of this picture Kilmarnock station appears to be in rather run-down condition and in dire need of a lick of paint. *Michael Allen*

The 4.16pm Kilmarnock to Glasgow St Enoch stopping train makes an energetic departure behind Class 2P 4-4-0 No.40597 on 29th June 1957. Note that the locomotive is in very presentable condition and has the name of the shed to which it was allocated painted on the buffer beam in traditional ScR style. Hurlford shed was located south of Kilmarnock station, adjacent to the main line to Carlisle. In the late 1950s almost half of this class was allocated to Glasgow (Corkerhill) shed and depots in Ayrshire for use on local passenger services in the area. *Colour-Rail*

The 11.56am to Kilmarnock eases out of Glasgow St Enoch station behind a beautifully turned out Stanier Class 5MT 4-6-0 No.45124 on 16th May 1964. St Enoch station was proposed by the City of Glasgow Union Railway, an alliance of various companies that operated in the city, and the idea was that the grand, new station would have impressive frontages in St Enoch Square and Argyle Street. Alas, some property had to be demolished before the promoters' dream could be realised and this delayed opening until 1st May 1876, the first day of through services to and from London via the Settle & Carlisle line. Passengers arriving off the first train from London could not fail to have been impressed by the splendour and size of the station, which boasted an 80ft. high, 504ft. long glazed arch with a clear span of 198ft. The premises were ceremonially opened by the Prince and Princess of Wales, who arrived in the Royal train on 17th October 1876. The magnificent St Enoch hotel welcomed its first guests on 3rd July 1879. Sadly, the contraction of the railway system led to the closure of St Enoch on 27th June 1966 from which date all remaining services south of the river Clyde were concentrated on Glasgow Central station. The last trains to serve St Enoch were formed of diesel units, the final steam arrival reportedly being the 9.00pm from Ayr on Saturday 25th June which produced BR Standard Class 5MT No.73120. *Michael Allen*

Ireland lured railway entrepreneurs and the short sea route was from the small port of Portpatrick, a mere 21 miles across the choppy waters from Donaghadee. Building westwards from Dumfries entailed the crossing of numerous rivers and desolate moorland while the approach from Ayr involved heavy gradients across the tableland of south Ayrshire. The first line to strike towards Portpatrick was the Castle Douglas & Dumfries Railway which opened on 7th November 1859. Meanwhile on 10th August 1857 the Portpatrick Railway had obtained an Act to continue from Castle Douglas and this long stretch opened as far as Stranraer on 12th March 1861, the extension to the harbour being brought into use on 1st October 1862. Portpatrick was reached on 28th August 1862, but a regular steamboat service to Ireland was delayed until 1868. Portpatrick's status as a passenger port was abruptly ended in 1874, however, when Stranraer harbour, located in the much more sheltered waters of Loch Ryan, came into use. In 1885 the Portpatrick Railway merged with the Wigtownshire Railway, which had built a local line to Whithorn, to form the Portpatrick & Wigtownshire Joint Railway, latterly better known as part of the Dumfries to Stranraer route. This line traversed wild and remote country and, furthermore, some of the stations were poorly sited in relation to the towns they were supposed to serve. The entire line lost its passenger service from 14th June 1965 when one of the most attractive but, perhaps, least known lines in Scotland faded into history. In this portrait an unidentified BR Standard Class 4MT 2-6-0 heads away from Dalbeattie with the 8.07am Dumfries to Kirkcudbright train on 22nd April 1965. *John Beckett*

DUMFRIES TO STRANRAER AND THE WHITHORN BRANCH

A Stranraer to Dumfries freight train, headed by Stanier Class 5MT 4-6-0 No.44883, approaches Castle Douglas on a bright 29th May 1965. Locomotives of this class predominated on the final day of services, with No.45480 on the Newcastle to Stranraer Harbour boat train (12.01pm from Dumfries) while sister engine No.45115 worked the corresponding train in the opposite direction, the 1.40pm from Stranraer. No.45480 later returned, in double harness with No.44689, on the *very last* 10.00pm Stranraer to London Euston boat train to be routed this way. BR Standard Class 4MT 2-6-0 No.76074 powered the 8.20am local train from Dumfries to Stranraer and the 3.35pm return service, while BR Standard 2-6-4T No.80117 hauled the 8.00am Stranraer to Dumfries, so another BR Standard class was represented on that fateful day. *Roy Patterson*

The public timetable stated quite clearly that there was 'no public access' available to Loch Skerrow station except, of course, for intrepid railway passengers! The station, which had basic facilities more akin to those of a halt, was located between Castle Douglas and Newton Stewart, on the southern shore of the loch of the same name, surrounded by bleak, open moors and forests, with no road access. For those seeking peace and solitude this was certainly the place to escape from the pressures of everyday life and it is likely that the station was used solely by walkers and fishermen. The train service advertised in the summer 1963 timetable was ideal for such people, with morning and evening trains in each direction, and there were even reasonable connections available from London Euston for those hardly individuals prepared to arrive on the last train and spend a night under canvas! Westbound trains faced a 1 in 80 climb for four miles before reaching Loch Skerrow so when the double-headed heavy overnight sleeping-car train from London was approaching the locomotive sounds must have been truly memorable as they echoed across the moors. This rare picture of the station was taken on 15th April 1963 when a rail tour headed by 'Jubilee' Class 6P5F 4-6-0 No.45588 *Kashmir* stopped briefly to take on water, this being one commodity that was plentiful at this remarkable railway outpost. One wonders how the signalman got there – perhaps he lived in an adjacent cottage. *Roy Denison*

A further view of the rather basic facilities provided at this remote outpost, showing the up platform, water crane with its accompanying brazier, and signal box. Note the solidly constructed fence, no doubt installed to deter all but the most adventurous sheep. *Gerald Daniels*

From the former Palnure station (closed 7th May 1951) to Gatehouse-of-Fleet eastbound trains faced almost seven miles of continuous climbing at 1 in 80 and in this picture BR Standard 'Clan' Class 6P5F Pacific No.72008 *Clan Macleod* and 'Black Five' No.45463 are seen battling their way up the bank through Creetown station on 29th May 1965 with (what appears to be) a heavy freight in tow. In the summer 1963 timetable Gatehouse-of-Fleet station was, apparently, only served by trains to Stranraer on Mondays, Fridays and Saturdays while in the other direction no services at all were advertised to call! This amazing situation is unlikely to have worried the inhabitants of the village unduly, however, because their station was about six miles distant and the village is located on a main road! *Roy Patterson*

The splendour of the scenery on the Dumfries to Stranraer line is clearly apparent from this illustration of BR Standard Class 4MT 2-6-4T No.80061 leaving Newton Stewart with the 3.35pm Stranraer Town to Dumfries train on 29th May 1965. It is sad to reflect that a little more than two weeks after this picture was taken this lovely line was closed. *Roy Patterson*

The 19¼ miles-long branch from Newton Stewart to Whithorn was opened in stages by the Wigtownshire Railway which was authorised in 1872. The first section, as far as Millisle, came into use on 2nd August 1875 while the line was opened throughout on 9th July 1877. There was also an obscure branch from Millisle to Garlieston which never carried regular passenger traffic but was used for excursions to the Isle of Man. The line to Whithorn served a very thinly populated area and passenger trains ceased as long ago as 25th September 1950. Goods traffic proved to be much more long lasting, the last trains running on 5th October 1964. In this view Class 2F 0-6-0 No.57340 is depicted heading southwards at Wigtown with a goods train for Whithorn in the early 1960s. *Gerald Daniels*

The train depicted in the previous photograph is seen again, this time pausing at the former Sorbie station, which was 13½ miles from Newton Stewart. Despite the fact that passenger services had been withdrawn some years before this picture was taken, the station building is still standing. The station here only served a tiny hamlet and is unlikely to have been busy at any time during its existence. Latterly, the goods train had run only thrice weekly so visiting photographers had to choose the day of their visit carefully, otherwise they may have been disappointed. *Gerald Daniels*

A general view of Stranraer Town station in May 1964 which, by the time of this photograph, was the 'end of the line' from Glasgow. The station was located on the south-eastern fringe of the town, hence the green fields on the right. Those over-optimistic souls who promoted lines to Stranraer really had their eyes on (what they hoped would become) the lucrative traffic to Ireland via Portpatrick harbour but they were destined to be disappointed when this business was transferred to Stranraer Harbour in 1874. The trackbed in the foreground is the course of the line to Portpatrick which was closed to passengers on 6th February 1950.
The late J.H. Moss / Stuart Ackley collection

The icy wastes of Barrhill! BR Standard Class 5MT 4-6-0 No.73009 pauses at Barrhill station with a train bound for Stranraer during the bitterly cold weather of January 1963. On 5th February 1963 the 5.10pm Glasgow to Stranraer diesel train became stuck in snowdrifts at Barrhill and some of the passengers had to be taken off by helicopter during the following day. During the ensuing days strenuous efforts were made to clear the line but these were obviously not entirely successful because some passengers bound for Ireland had to be taken to Stranraer via Mauchline and Dumfries. It is recorded that on 15th February No.73009 took a short train from Ayr to Stranraer via Dumfries for the benefit of people *en route* to Ireland. Another week elapsed before the line was fully operational again. *Colour-Rail*

STRANRAER TO GLASGOW (ST ENOCH)

Two heads of steam are better than one, especially on the very steeply graded Ayr to Stranraer line! South of Girvan trains bound for Stranraer face a 3½ miles-long bank graded at 1 in 54/56 while between Pinwherry and Glenwhilly there is an 8½ miles-long climb mostly at 1 in 67/73, so this route was not one for faint-hearted enginemen. Here, a heavy, unidentified southbound train speeds southwards near Dalrymple in June 1966. Motive power is provided by a brace of 'Black Fives', the leading engine being No.45167. *Roy Hobbs*

The 41½ miles-long section between Glasgow and Ayr was built by the GPK&AR, who obtained an Act on 15th July 1837. Construction of the line involved few engineering works of note and, unusually for a Scottish line, much of the route was totally flat. This stretch was opened in stages, through running commencing on 12th August 1840. The push southwards from Ayr commenced with the opening of the Ayr & Maybole Railway, freight trains running from 15th September 1856 with passenger services starting a month later. Girvan was reached by the Maybole & Girvan Railway on 24th May 1860. Portpatrick remained the goal of the railway pioneers however, but the terrain and lack of population south of Girvan deterred all but the most optimistic promoters. Ten years elapsed before the 30 miles-long Girvan & Portpatrick Junction Railway opened for traffic on 5th October 1870. In this picture BR Standard Class 4MT 2-6-4T No.80112 sits in one of the bay platforms at Ayr in August 1963. *Roy Denison*

The line to Wemyss Bay, which diverged from the main Glasgow to Greenock line at Port Glasgow, was opened by the Greenock & Wemyss Bay Railway company on 13th May 1865 and offered through rail and steamboat connections between Glasgow (Bridge Street Station) and the Clyde coast resorts. The company remained nominally independent until it was amalgamated with the Caledonian Railway on 1st August 1893. Regrettably, no pictures of steam trains on this route were submitted for inclusion in this album but here are two views of the magnificent Wemyss Bay station building, opened in 1903. This shot, taken on 12th April 1963, shows the exterior with the sixty-foot-high clock tower. The station was built in the Queen Anne style, half-timbered and roughcast with sandstone facing. *Michael Allen*

The station, undoubtedly an architectural gem, was designed by James Miller for the Caledonian Railway and has a really exquisite interior which features a large, circular steel and glass roof. The station became renowned for its outstanding displays of potted plants and hanging baskets, some being visible in this picture taken on 1st June 1963. *John Langford*

WEMYSS BAY STATION

The station and pier at Gourock were opened by the Caledonian Railway on 1st June 1889. Construction of the line involved boring a very long tunnel under Greenock so it must have been a costly exercise for the CR, but one that later reaped huge dividends, such was the growth of Glasgow commuter traffic. This shot was taken at Gourock on 25th May 1965 and shows BR Standard Class 4MT No.80001 apparently stabled between duties. The ship berthed at the quay in the middle of the picture is the *Duchess of Montrose* which was built by Denny Bros. of Dumbarton in 1930 and was used on sailings from Gourock to Inveraray and other local piers. It made its last commercial sailing on 30th August 1964, subsequently being laid up at Gourock until September 1965 when it departed on its last journey to a shipbreaker's yard in Belgium. *Alan Chandler*

The 10.40am Gourock to Glasgow (Central) train, powered by Fairburn Class 4MT 2-6-4T No.42058, waits at Paisley (Gilmour Street) before setting off on the last lap of its journey. This train stopped at only four stations during its 26¼ miles-long run and the journey time was forty-four minutes. This picture was taken on 13th April 1963. In 1966, the penultimate year of steam traction in Scotland, the highest concentration of steam-worked passenger trains was on the Gourock to Glasgow line, BR Standard Class 4MT 2-6-4Ts being predominant. *Michael Allen*

The first idea for a railway to Fort William was made in the early 1880s by the Glasgow & North Western Railway, who proposed a route to Inverness via Crianlarich, Rannoch Moor, Glencoe, Fort William and the Great Glen. The bill failed after a protracted parliamentary battle, much to the disappointment of Fort William residents who had campaigned vigorously for the line. In 1884, however, a Royal Commission was set up under Lord Napier to investigate the crofting system and this concluded that the remoteness of the Highlands was responsible for many of the region's economic and social problems. The West Highland Railway project, backed by the NBR, proposed a different route to that previously suggested which would approach Fort William from Glen Spean and continue to a steamer terminal and fishing base at Roshven on Loch Ailort. The latter idea did not meet with universal approval, however, and was abandoned, but the main plan for a line to Fort William was passed by Parliament in 1889. The first sod was cut by Lord Abinger in Fort William and work proceeded at four other locations, but mounting construction costs almost brought about the financial collapse of the company which was only saved by the intervention of J.H. Renton Esq., a wealthy man who was one of the directors. The line was opened throughout from Helensburgh on 7th August 1894. Here, former NBR Class J37 0-6-0 No.64558 is seen at Garelochhead in May 1959 with a pick-up goods train serving only the southern end of the line. *Colour-Rail*

The heavy gradients on the section of the West Highland line north of Crianlarich are severe, but almost equally demanding is the climb up to Glen Douglas (564 feet above sea level) between Garelochhead and Arrochar & Tarbet. Northbound trains face six miles of continuous climbing from Garelochhead, varying between 1 in 54 and 1 in 132, while in the southbound direction the ascent is even more demanding, with four miles at 1 in 57, apart from a brief, more moderate section at Glen Douglas Halt. In this illustration Stanier Class 5MT 4-6-0 No.44976 is depicted waiting to cross a northbound train at remote Glen Douglas on 15th June 1959. The tiny halt here was approached by a farm track, the nearest road being a quarter of a mile distant; it was closed from 15th June 1964. *Derek Penney*

The wayside stations at the southern end of the West Highland line were served by a local service that plied between Craigendoran and Arrochar & Tarbet, motive power latterly being former NBR C15 Class 4-4-2Ts working push-pull trains. Thirty of these machines were constructed by the Yorkshire Engine Co. Ltd between 1911 and 1913 for NBR passenger services and most were scrapped in the mid-1950s. Three examples were fitted with push-pull apparatus and two of these, Nos. 67460 and 67474, outlived the other engines by several years. In this shot the latter engine, in lovely external condition, is seen at Arrochar & Tarbet on 15th June 1959, a brilliantly sunny day. Note the vacuum and air control pipes (for push-pull working) on the locomotive's buffer beam and the Westinghouse air pump. The photographer was on holiday 'north of the border' at the time and states that seeing and photographing these survivors at work was his top priority. Sure enough, this was their last full year in service, so he definitely got his priorities right! He photographed the other surviving member of the class at Eastfield shed. *Derek Penney*

On 8th/9th May 1959 BBC Television cameramen descended on the West Highland line to undertake some filming for the 'Railway Roundabout' programme. In connection with this work a brace of NBR D34 Class 'Glen' 4-4-0s, Nos.62471 *Glen Falloch* and 62496 *Glen Loy*, were specially rostered to work the 5.45am Glasgow (Queen Street) to Mallaig as far as Fort William and 2.56pm *ex*-Fort William return train. Both engines had been beautifully prepared, each having red coupling rods while the front of the leading engine was adorned with silver paint. No.62477 *Glen Dochart* was reportedly patched up and cleaned in case one of the veterans faltered. A trial run, on the trains mentioned above, had been made on 28th April to assess the capabilities of the pair. The two locomotives are pictured at Ardlui on 9th May 1959 bathed in glorious morning sunshine. What an absolutely magnificent sight! *Colour-Rail*

Passengers aboard the 10.21am Glasgow (Queen Street) to Mallaig train stretch their legs at Crianlarich (Upper) station on 8th September 1958 as the sun shines through a break in the clouds. Note the colourful flower beds and carriages in the carmine and cream livery which could still be seen at that time but was being phased out in favour of maroon. *Gerald Daniels*

Breathtaking, unsurpassed and spectacular are just a few of the superlatives that have been used over the years to describe the absolutely magnificent section of the West Highland line between Crianlarich and Tulloch. For southbound trains in steam days it was one long, continuous slog, mostly at 1 in 55, from Bridge of Orchy to the summit situated two miles or so north of Tyndrum (Upper) station. Here, Stanier Class 5MT 4-6-0 No.44996 emits a pall of black smoke across the moors (and, no doubt, the adjacent A82 main road) as it heaves the 12 noon Mallaig to Glasgow (Queen Street) train up the final stretch of the climb to County March summit on 12th September 1959. *Colour-Rail*

On 18th August 1959 the 1.00pm Mallaig to Glasgow train was composed of only six coaches which would have presented no problems at all, even on a steep gradient, for the extremely powerful combination of 'Black Five' 4-6-0 No.44968 piloted by BR Standard Class 5MT 4-6-0 No.73077. The former engine even appears to be 'blowing off' slightly. In this picture the pair are seen negotiating the Horseshoe Curve, north of Tyndrum (Upper), which, for many travellers, is the highlight of a journey on this outstanding route. Note that the fifth vehicle in the train is a Gresley-designed restaurant car. *Colour-Rail*

Opposite: The delightful pairing of D34 Class 4-4-0s Nos. 62496 *Glen Loy* and 62471 *Glen Falloch* is seen again, this time photographed from the train threading the scenic Monessie Gorge, between Tulloch and Roy Bridge, with the 2.56pm Fort William to Glasgow on 9th May 1959. The railway runs on a ledge cut into the side of the gorge, giving passengers a splendid view of the foaming waters of the river Spean as they tumble over huge boulders strewn across the river bed. Unfortunately, on the day of this photograph there was very little water to be seen, the river presumably being very low after a dry spell of weather. The two 'Glens' performed excellently, keeping time throughout and steaming very freely, the only slight headache for those in charge being the tendency of *Glen Loy*'s bearings to become warm especially on the last homeward journey. Perhaps it was just as well that Nos. 62496 and 62471 performed faultlessly because the reserve engine, No.62477 *Glen Dochart,* apparently failed, being noted out of steam, facing southwards, in a siding at Corrour on the morning of Saturday 9th May. *Colour-Rail*

The coming of the railways to the Highlands often met with opposition from landowners, but by the time the West Highland line had reached Fort William the advantages of rail transport were becoming clear and there was only token opposition when the Mallaig extension was proposed. The bill was passed in 1894 but financial wrangling caused a two-year delay and the original contractor was forced to withdraw. This left the way open for Robert 'Concrete Bob' McAlpine who took just over four years to finish the job rather than the five years anticipated. Hutted camps were provided at Fort William and Lochailort for the navvies engaged upon building the line, stores apparently being managed by a grocery firm in Glasgow. There were two substantial civil engineering works, the bridge over Borrowdale burn, between Beasdale and Arisaig, and construction of Glenfinnan viaduct which, even today, is probably one of Robert McAlpine's best-known achievements. The former involved a 127ft arch and was, at least for a time, the world's longest concrete span. Steamers and trains converged on the tiny village of Mallaig when the line opened on 1st April 1901 – a really great day for the 'locals' and the fishing community in particular. In this portrait Class K2 2-6-0 No.61784, in highly polished condition, is depicted at Fort William with the 5.45am Glasgow (Queen Street) to Mallaig on 9th May 1959. This was one of the days when the two 'Glens' powered the 5.45am train by arrangement with the BBC who were filming, so passengers were privileged to have some really attractive motive power but one wonders how many appreciated the fact. *Colour-Rail*

A pair of canoes on the platform, a fine example of Highland topiary, an attractive signal box complete with a tall lower quadrant signal and crossing gates over a local lane ... it is difficult to believe this is how the little station at Banavie, just outside Fort William, used to look. In this picture the photographer has 'timed' his shot perfectly and caught the signalman in classic pose exchanging the tokens with the fireman of Class B1 4-6-0 No.61352 working the 12.30pm Mallaig to Glasgow train on 2nd September 1961. There used to be a short branch to Banavie Pier which opened on 1st June 1895 but was closed to passengers when the Second World War was declared in September 1939 and never reopened. Goods trains continued to run until 6th August 1951. *Gerald Daniels*

The massive concrete viaduct at Glenfinnan is one of the major landmarks on the Fort Willam to Mallaig line which was, as previously stated, built by McAlpine and his men. The 416 yards-long structure consists of twenty-one arches and has a maximum height of 100 feet. In this picture, taken from the fifth coach of the 5.45am Glasgow (Queen Street) to Mallaig train, Class K2 No.61784 can be seen heading across this impressive feat of engineering towards Glenfinnan station on 9th May 1959. *Colour-Rail*

Photographed on an overcast day which is so typical, alas, of the weather conditions in the western Highlands, a pair of Class K1 2-6-0s, Nos.62034 and 62012, attempts to gather speed after departure from Lochailort station with a Glasgow-bound train on 27th July 1957. Between Lochailort and Glenfinnan the railway line skirts the southern shore of Loch Eilt, one of the most picturesque sections on the Fort William to Mallaig route.
Colour-Rail

Many of the stations on the West Highland line are situated in beautiful surroundings, but, perhaps, the tiny station at Lochailort is the most dramatically located of all, virtually surrounded by towering mountains. This scene was recorded on 16th August 1963 and shows the station bathed in sunshine, while the mountains beyond are largely in cloud shadow. This is a lonely spot with only a few scattered houses in the immediate vicinity and waiting here for a train on a wet and windy night, often with only the flickering oil lamps for company, must have been quite an experience. If their train failed to materialise prospective passengers could, as a last resort, always thumb a lift from a passing motorist (if there were any!) on the adjacent road. *Roy Denison*

Passengers make their way to the steamers at Mallaig as Class K2 2-6-0 No.61784 carries out a little light shunting near the quay in May 1959. A local lad with time on his hands looks on as the locomotive potters around. One wonders how the authorities would react today to members of the public ambling along so close to shunting operations. Apart from the dangers posed by moving vehicles, the ground seems to be a trifle uneven, thus creating 'trip' hazards, and, who knows, perhaps the crane's jib was about to swing into action any second. Then there was the chance of people being scalded by escaping steam, stepping on a hot cinder from the engine's ashpan or falling off the edge of the quay into the uninviting waters of the Sound of Sleat. But nobody worried because at that time people simply took much more responsibility for their own personal safety. How we may ask, in these health and safety conscious times, did people survive? *Colour-Rail*

An unidentified Class B1 4-6-0 lurks in the background of this portrait of Mallaig station which is believed to date from the early 1960s. In addition to being a fishing port, Mallaig is the departure point for the boats to Armadale on the Isle of Skye and the small islands of Canna, Rhum and Eigg. The sunlight casts fascinating shadows as a fair number of people mingle on the platforms: perhaps a train was about to depart. Platform barrows are strewn around in the usual fashion while behind the display board with its colourful posters there is (what seems to be) a tractor. One wonders how many passengers responded to the posters advertising the attractions of the Isle of Wight and Norfolk! Regrettably, the decorative twin gabled glazed canopies, which gave passengers protection from the violent gales that sweep in off the sea, were subsequently demolished leaving only bare and featureless platforms. How desperately sad! *The late K. Bannister / Stuart Ackley collection*

In the late 1950s the Scottish Region made the enlightened decision to return four veteran locomotives to traffic in pre-grouping livery, mainly for use on special workings. One engine from each of the pre-grouping Scottish companies was selected, apart from the Glasgow & South Western Railway whose locomotives had been withdrawn before nationalisation. The locomotives concerned were used principally on enthusiasts' specials and gave much pleasure to the enthusiast fraternity plus ordinary members of the public with only a passing interest in railways. In this photograph, former Great North of Scotland Railway 4-4-0 No.49 *Gordon Highlander* passes Cobbinshaw station (closed in April 1966), between Midcalder and Carstairs, with the 'Scottish Rambler No.4' special on 19th April 1965. This machine was one of eight locomotives built by the North British Locomotive Company in 1920 to the design of T.E. Heywood and known as Class F. The expanse of water in the background could easily be mistaken for a loch but is actually a reservoir. *Roy Hobbs*

One wonders what was going through the mind of the guard as he stands beside the Caledonian Railway 'Single' locomotive No.123 at remote Killin Junction on 11th April 1963. Perhaps he was wondering whether he was going to be able to return his passengers to 'civilisation' in such blizzard conditions. The train is the Easter 1963 'Scottish Rambler' *en route* from Glasgow to Crianlarich via Callander and back to Glasgow via the West Highland line. A few minutes before this shot was taken No.123, hauling the two preserved Caledonian Railway coaches, had been struggling up the 1 in 60 climb between Balquhidder and the summit at Glenoglehead crossing which is 941ft. above sea level. Built in 1886 by Neilson & Co., No.123 had a colourful career and took part in the 'Race to the North' in 1888 before being allocated less stressful duties hauling the directors' saloon in the 1920s. In 1930 it briefly returned to everyday service, normally working between Perth and Dundee, before being withdrawn from ordinary traffic in 1935. It was restored for special use in 1958, even venturing down to the Bluebell Railway in Sussex in 1963. Two years later it was retired to the Glasgow Transport Museum. *Ken Falconer*

A scene at Burghead, on the former Alves to Hopeman branch, showing Highland Railway 4-6-0 No.103 leaving with a rail tour on 21st April 1962. The branch lost its passenger service from 14th September 1931 but goods traffic to Burghead continued for many years thereafter, thus enabling the occasional special to run down the branch. The section beyond Burghead to Hopeman was closed completely, however, from 30th December 1957. No.103 was the first 4-6-0 to appear in Great Britain, being built to the design of David Jones and out-shopped by Sharp Stewart in 1894. The locomotive was set aside for preservation in 1934 and was restored to working order for special trains in 1959, being repainted in Stroudley's 'improved engine green' which was actually a vivid yellow colour! *Roy Hobbs*

Former North British Railway 4-4-0 No.256 *Glen Douglas* is the last of our quartet of delightful Scottish preserved locomotives. It is one of a class of thirty-two engines built at Cowlairs in 1913-20, this particular locomotive being constructed in September 1913. *Glen Douglas* was not withdrawn from stock in the usual way but was given a thorough overhaul at Cowlairs Works, reportedly emerging from the works in resplendent condition on 24th July 1959. Rather belatedly, perhaps, it was officially re-numbered in November 1959. In this picture it is seen at Auchtermuchty, on the former Ladybank to Mawcarse Junction line in Fife, with a special train on 13th April 1963. This line suffered the withdrawal of its passenger trains from 5th June 1950, but remained open for goods traffic. *Roy Hobbs*

In this photograph, which was taken on 13th April 1963, Stanier 'Black Five' No.45359 is seen entering Buchanan Street station with the 7.52am from Callander, formed entirely of LMSR-designed coaching stock. Judging by the condensation on the carriage windows it seems to have been a cold morning, but at least it was bright! The principal long distance services that used Buchanan Street station were those to Inverness, Aberdeen and Oban while, on occasions, trains to and from the south were diverted there owing to engineering works on the normal route into Glasgow Central. There was a huge goods depot adjacent to the station premises, this reputedly being the largest on the Scottish Region. The station, which latterly had become very dingy and dilapidated, was closed on 7th November 1966 when the remaining services were diverted to Queen Street station. Buchanan Street station was not the most attractive place to start a railway journey and one wonders how many city terminal stations were dominated by a huge cooling tower! *Michael Allen*

The magnificent landscape through which the Glasgow to Oban line passed justified its position as one of Scotland's epic routes but, sadly, the section between Dunblane and Crianlarich (Lower), which traversed some particularly rugged and wild terrain, was closed in 1965 when services were diverted to run via the West Highland line as far as Crianlarich (Upper). The first section of the route, from Dunblane to Callander, was opened by the delightfully named Dunblane, Doune & Callander Railway on 1st July 1858. The rest of the line was built by the Callander & Oban Railway which gained parliamentary approval in 1865, but progress was painfully slow, the opening as far as Killin (later known as Glenoglehead) taking place on 1st June 1870. The line opened to Tyndrum in August 1873 and at one time it seemed likely that it would have to be abandoned at that point due to chronic financial difficulties. The company's general manager, John Anderson, was determined that any setback would be temporary, however, and construction was later resumed with the result that Dalmally was reached in 1877, while on 30th June 1880 the company at long last achieved its goal when trains started running to and from Oban. Here, on a bright and clear 3rd April 1961, Stanier Class 5MT No.44718 waits to leave Callander with the 7.50am Glasgow (Buchanan Street) to Oban train. *Roy Patterson*

Another 'Black Five' at Callander, these engines being common performers on the Oban line services. In this picture Class 5MT No.44798 is depicted running into the station with an Oban to Glasgow train in July 1958. Note that the train comprises a rake of LMSR-designed coaches, including (what appears to be) a vintage specimen towards the rear. The first two coaches are in carmine and cream livery which was very much in vogue at that time. The mountainous background gives a hint of the absolutely outstanding landscape in this area. *Colour-Rail*

A nine-coach Oban to Glasgow train comprised of an assortment of carriages approaches Balquhidder on 27th July 1957; Stanier Class 5MT 4-6-0 No.44922 is in charge. Here was the junction for the rather remote cross-country line to Comrie, Crieff and Perth, the section west of Comrie being promoted by the Comrie, St Fillans and Lochearnhead Railway which opened to Balquhidder on 1st May 1905. This line traversed very sparsely populated country and the section from Comrie to Balquhidder was closed as early as 1st October 1951, the Crieff to Perth stretch also closing on the same day. So, Balquhidder's junction status was relatively short-lived. *Colour-Rail*

Set amongst the grandeur of towering mountains on all sides the small hamlet of Crianlarich was well provided with railway services out of all proportion to its size. Prospective passengers could choose to travel to Glasgow via Dunblane from Crianlarich (Lower) station or take the West Highland train to Glasgow via Helensburgh from the Upper station. This shot, taken at Crianlarich West Junction in June 1965, shows the Dunblane to Oban line in the left foreground with BR Standard Class 4MT 2-6-4T No.80028 doing a spot of shunting, possibly between duties on the nearby Killin branch. On the right is the chord that was opened between Crianlarich (Upper) and West Junction on 20th December 1897 but not used for regular passenger trains until 23rd May 1949. In the middle distance a slender girder bridge takes the West Highland line across the river Fillan. Today Glasgow to Oban trains travel via the West Highland line and gain their original route to Oban using the chord line seen here. *Colour-Rail*

In this illustration Stanier 'Black Five' No.45396 is seen taking a Glasgow to Oban train along the shore of Loch Awe in the summer of 1961. This is one of the very few stretches of the route which is level, so the enginemen would have been able to take things relatively easy – at least for a few miles. Between Loch Awe and the next major intermediate station, Taynuilt, the line threads the Pass of Brander on a ledge cut along the foot of Ben Cruachan. This section presented considerable difficulties during construction, falling boulders being a constant hazard, and in 1881 several coaches were derailed by rockfalls down the boulder strewn mountainside. A wire fence that gave warning of falling rocks was installed, an audible warning being made automatically following any breakage of the wire. There was even a special grade of signal watchman for the men employed to monitor the system which was known as 'Anderson's piano' because the wind whistling through the wires produced a musical humming noise.
Michael Mensing

GLASGOW (BUCHANAN STREET) TO OBAN

A brace of Stanier Class 5MT 4-6-0s, Nos.44925 and 45013, appear to be making light work of hauling the 12 noon Glasgow (Buchanan Street) to Oban train up the 1 in 72/61 gradient through Strath Fillan between Crianlarich (Lower) and Tyndrum (Lower). Both locomotives are 'blowing off' and the lack of smoke indicates that their firemen were doing a competent job. The West Highland line is out of sight running on a ledge on the mountainside on the left. This picture was taken on 12th September 1959. *Colour-Rail*

The massive bulk of Ben Cruachan (3,695 feet above sea level) looms in the distance as the fireman of Stanier Class 5MT No.45357 pulls the rod to open the water tank valve so his locomotive can take water. This photograph was taken at Taynuilt on 17th May 1960. Freight traffic on the Oban line consisted of the usual general merchandise and in addition there was considerable fish traffic from Oban, this being forwarded in specially insulated containers. Fuel oil for local use and on the various islands served by ferries from Oban was also a major commodity conveyed by the railway. Note the delightful lower quadrant signals at this location. *Michael Mensing*

Above: A panoramic view of Oban station and some of the surrounding area: this picture probably dates from the early 1960s. Two vintage buses add interest to the scene. The original station building was an architectural treasure with an impressive clock tower, but it was demolished by BR in the mid-1980s and replaced by a characterless modern structure which was brought into use in January 1986. The two platforms without canopies visible on the right of the picture were installed in 1904 following the opening of the branch from Ballachulish. At one time Oban had two signal boxes, the old goods junction box closing in May 1969 while the larger station signal box lasted until 5th December 1982, from which date semaphore signalling was eliminated. *The late J. H. Moss / Stuart Ackley collection*

Opposite upper: The distinctive outline of Connel Ferry bridge in the background immediately identifies the location of this picture which was taken about one mile east of Connel Ferry station on a sunny 24th May 1960. The train is the 12.05pm Oban to Glasgow Buchanan Street and a brace of Stanier 'Black Fives', Nos.45356 and 45047, provide the motive power. The waters of Loch Etive form an attractive backdrop. *Michael Mensing*

Opposite lower: The waters of Oban bay form a pleasant background as a rather dirty former Caledonian Railway Class 2P 0-4-4T, No.55124, undertakes a little light shunting on 18th May 1961. At that time the railway system still operated with an amazing collection of rolling stock as evidenced here by the variety of vehicles on view even at this far-flung outpost of the network. A former Southern Railway parcels van is immediately behind the locomotive, followed by a goods brake van with a Thompson-designed suburban coach on the rear. The latter would have been used on the Ballachulish branch trains. In the siding in front of the shed there is a former Pullman car, presumably in use as a dining car on the Glasgow trains while some former LMSR coaches are visible on the extreme right of the shot. *Michael Mensing*

GLASGOW (BUCHANAN STREET) TO OBAN

Construction of the Killin Junction to Loch Tay branch was primarily instigated by the Marquis of Breadalbane after his efforts to persuade the Callander & Oban Railway to provide a rail link from the main Dunblane to Oban line, to connect with the Loch Tay steamers, had come to nothing. The five miles-long line was authorised by Parliament in 1883 and opened to traffic on 13th March 1886. A new station, known as Killin Junction, was built on the main line to enable passengers to transfer on to the branch. In more recent years it was shown in the timetables as an exchange platform only. The line north of Killin to Loch Tay was closed to passengers on 11th September 1939, but the locomotive shed was located there so it remained in use to provide access. The branch was worked by Caledonian Railway 0-4-4Ts for many years until BR Standard 2-6-4Ts were introduced. The passenger service on the main line between Dunblane and Crianlarich, which was used by Glasgow to Oban trains, was due to be withdrawn from 1st November 1965 with services being diverted to run via the West Highland line. The branch service was also due to be axed from the same date. In the event a rock fall in Glen Ogle on 28th September 1965 caused the train service to be prematurely suspended and buses laid on until the official closure date. Snow is still visible on the mountain tops as Class 2P 0-4-4T No.55217 waits to leave Killin with the 11.05am branch working to Killin Junction on 3rd April 1961. *Roy Patterson*

There were not many branch lines in the Scottish Highlands but those few that were built were surely in a class of their own. This masterpiece of a picture shows BR Standard Class 4MT 2-6-4T No.80092 puffing along with a branch train bound for Killin Junction on 6th May 1965. Could one wish for better scenery than the fabulous landscape seen here? What a shame the sun did not deign to shine. The exceptional cleanliness of the locomotive was not, apparently, due to a change of BR engine cleaning policy(!), but the efforts of a group of visiting enthusiasts who did not want a filthy locomotive to spoil their pictures! *Roy Hobbs*

The branch from Oban (Connel Ferry) to Ballachulish was promoted by the Callander & Oban Railway and it was originally intended to take the line through to Fort William, in conjunction with the North British Railway, by means of a bridge over Loch Leven. The idea of continuing to Fort William met with considerable local opposition, however, and had to be abandoned. The rest of the scheme proceeded and the Ballachulish branch was opened for traffic on 24th August 1903. It is recorded that on the opening day visitors were treated to a ride on the railway plus an excursion to Glencoe, the terminal station being known as 'Ballachulish (Glencoe)'. In this picture, taken at Oban station on 17th May 1960, Class 2P 0-4-4T No.55238 poses with the empty stock of the 3.57pm from Ballachulish before drawing it out of the station. On the right a Swindon-built 3-car 'Cross-Country' unit is waiting to return to Glasgow with an excursion working. *Michael Mensing*

BALLACHULISH BRANCH

Trains leaving Oban face what might be mildly described as a 'challenging start' away from the terminus, three miles of unrelenting 1 in 50 gradient as far as Glencruitten crossing. In this picture the 4.55pm from Oban to Ballachulish is seen bustling up to the summit at Glencruitten (310 feet above sea level) behind Class 2P 0-4-4T No.55124 on 18th May 1961. *Michael Mensing*

BALLACHULISH BRANCH

'Toll Bridge – One Way Traffic'. 'Warning – Stop at red light ring bell and wait for green light'. Generations of motorists travelling from Oban to Ballachulish in the past doubtless moaned about the regulations that had to be obeyed before they could cross Connel Ferry Bridge but one wonders how many realised that it was originally constructed primarily as a railway bridge and trains always had priority. The bridge was built with road traffic in mind, but the local authority was in dispute with the railway over the methods of charging tolls and some years elapsed before agreement was reached and road vehicles were able to cross. Construction of the 1,044 feet-long cantilever bridge across Loch Etive began in 1898 with the masonry abutments and piers, while the steelwork was erected from 1900 to 1903. Nearly 2,600 tons of steel were required for the main span. Crossing the bridge may have been a bit of a performance for motorists but at least it saved a 35 miles-long detour. This picture was taken in the early 1960s when trains were still operating over the bridge. *Michael Mensing*

Duror was one of the small wayside stations on the Ballachulish branch and in this view former Caledonian Railway Class 2P 0-4-4T No.55263 is seen waiting in the sunshine to resume its journey southwards to Oban on 5th May 1959. There used to be a loop here but it had long since been taken out by the time of this photograph. The branch ran alongside Loch Linnhe for much of its distance and offered breathtaking views across the loch to distant mountains, and would have been a strong challenger as the most scenic branch line in Great Britain. *Gerald Daniels*

The splendid scenery surrounding Ballachulish on the banks of Loch Leven is clearly evident from this picture of Class 2P 0-4-4T No.55238 waiting to leave with a two-coach train to Oban during the summer of 1960. There was a small, wooden locomotive shed at Ballachulish which was a sub-shed of Oban and, presumably, the engine working the first train of the day stabled there overnight. The line served a very thinly populated area and the train service advertised in the summer 1963 timetable consisted of a mere three return trains on Mondays to Fridays whilst an extra working was provided on Saturdays. The journey time for the 34 miles-long trip was around 1½ hours so passengers certainly had plenty of time to admire the wonderful scenery. The branch was closed completely from 28th March 1966 and one wonders how many motorists driving across the Connel Ferry Bridge today realise that it was also a railway bridge in times gone by. *Michael Mensing*

BALLACHULISH BRANCH

The 28 miles-long branch from Lenzie Junction, on the Glasgow to Edinburgh via Falkirk line, was opened in stages between 1848 and 1882, the first section as far as Lennoxtown being brought into use on 5th July 1848. The next stretch, the 9¾ miles-long section from Lennoxtown to Killearn, was opened on 1st July 1867. The final piece of line on to Aberfoyle was not brought into use until fifteen years later, on 1st October 1882. This used a section of track between Gartness Junction and Buchlyvie that had already been completed, in 1856 by the Forth & Clyde Junction Railway, so perhaps the long delay was caused by shortage of funds. There was a single platform terminus at Aberfoyle, an engine shed – latterly a sub-shed of Glasgow (Eastfield) – and a goods shed. In more prosperous times the LNER ran a coach service to the Trossachs but this ceased in September 1939 on the outbreak of war. The summer 1951 timetable reveals that a very meagre service of two trains a day each way operated on Mondays to Fridays with an extra working each way on Saturdays. The passenger service was withdrawn from 1st October 1951 while goods traffic north of Campsie Glen (just north of Lennoxtown) continued until 5th October 1959. The remnants of the line northwards from Lenzie were closed to all traffic from 4th April 1966. In this illustration Class J37 0-6-0 No.64580 is depicted shunting at Aberfoyle on 27th July 1958, by which time the well-maintained station building was presumably in private hands. *Colour-Rail*

The 10.00am Glasgow (Buchanan Street) to Inverness train, with Stanier Class 5MT 4-6-0 No.44980 in charge as far as Perth, is depicted climbing towards St Rollox shed on 15th April 1963. The shed was located on the other side of the road bridge from where the shot was taken, but it should be noted that St Rollox station was much nearer the city centre, about a mile north-east of Buchanan Street, and at one time was served by trains to and from Hamilton. At the time of this photograph there was a maze of tracks in this area which provided links to other lines in the city and St Rollox locomotive works, the signal box in the background marking the site of Germiston Junction where the line to Rutherglen diverged. Note the Buffet Restaurant Car formed immediately behind the engine – hardly an ideal arrangement. *Michael Allen*

Some of the best scenery on the Glasgow to Perth section can be found around Gleneagles where a range of hills forms a distant backdrop, although it has to be admitted that they do not quite match the grandeur of the Highlands. In this shot, taken on 20th May 1965, the 4.25pm Glasgow to Inverness train is seen approaching Gleneagles behind Gresley A4 Class Pacific No.60019 *Bittern*. It is unlikely that this working was rostered for steam traction and possible that *Bittern* was a last-minute substitute for a failed diesel. On arrival at Perth the coaches from Glasgow would have been coupled to the portion from Edinburgh and the train presumably taken forward by the diesel locomotive that had brought in the Edinburgh coaches. One wonders how *Bittern*'s crew would have reacted if they had been asked to work the train on to Inverness, along a very steeply graded route where one of these A4 Class thoroughbreds would have been somewhat out of place. *Alan Chandler*

GLASGOW (BUCHANAN STREET) TO INVERNESS

The principal section of the Highland main line, from Perth (Stanley Junction) to Aviemore, ran in splendid isolation from the rest of the system, the only junction being at Ballinluig where the branch from Aberfeldy joined the main line. In this illustration former Caledonian Railway Class 2P 0-4-4T No.55218 simmers in the branch platform after arrival with the 12 noon mixed train from Aberfeldy on 7th July 1959. Closure of the branch occurred on 3rd May 1965, from which date Ballinluig station was also closed. *Michael Allen*

The original route from Perth to Inverness was via Forres and the cutting of the first sod for the Perth & Inverness Railway took place there in October 1861. Despite the extremely inhospitable terrain and, no doubt, atrocious weather conditions, construction proceeded remarkably quickly, the line opening throughout to Dunkeld in September 1863. The section south of Dunkeld had been opened by the Perth & Dunkeld Railway in April 1856. The stretch between Aviemore and Inverness via Carr Bridge came on the scene much later, not opening throughout until November 1898. Today, this forms part of the main line between Perth and Inverness, the Aviemore to Forres route via Dava having succumbed to closure in October 1965. The Highland main line was converted to diesel operation in the early 1960s and consequently few pictures taken in the steam era were submitted for publication in this book. This shot of Dalnaspidal station's down platform was taken in snowy conditions from the 11.00am Inverness to Glasgow/Edinburgh train on 30th January 1960 and gives a hint of the freezing weather often experienced in the Highlands. For the record, motive power was a brace of 'Black Fives', Nos.45492 and 44978, and, despite the weather, the train arrived at Perth two minutes before time. *John Langford*

The notice board marking the summit of the line just north of Dalnaspidal station (which was closed from 3rd May 1965). Strangely, there was no mention that the summit was the highest point reached by a main line railway in Great Britain. This picture was taken on 18th May 1965. *Alan Chandler*

The name Culloden will forever be associated with a battle, but the crews of the 'Black Fives' seen here would have had an altogether different battle on their minds – the unrelenting slog up to Slochd summit – as they attacked the 'foothills' of the ascent just outside Inverness. The climb commences just after Millburn Junction (where the line to Aberdeen, which is just visible on the left, diverges) and continues, almost unbroken, mostly at 1 in 60/70, until the summit is reached at 1,315 feet above sea level. The train depicted is the 8.30am from Inverness to Edinburgh (Waverley), hauled by Nos.45192 and 45496, and this shot was taken on 23rd August 1959. *Colour-Rail*

The nameboard immediately identifies the location of this photograph, the station seen here being the terminus of the 8¾ miles-long branch from Ballinluig on the Perth to Inverness main line. The Aberfeldy branch was built under an Act obtained in 1861 and opened to passengers on 3rd July 1865. There was an intermediate station at Grandtully and in December 1935 the LMSR opened an additional halt at Balnaguard to serve a local estate. The passenger service generally consisted of six trains on weekdays, at least one of which provided the luxury of through coaches to Perth, even in BR days. Former Caledonian Railway 0-4-4T No.55200 is seen at Aberfeldy in May 1959 on one of the mixed trains that were a feature of the line. This delightful backwater was closed from 3rd May 1965, so it just missed its centenary. *Colour-Rail*

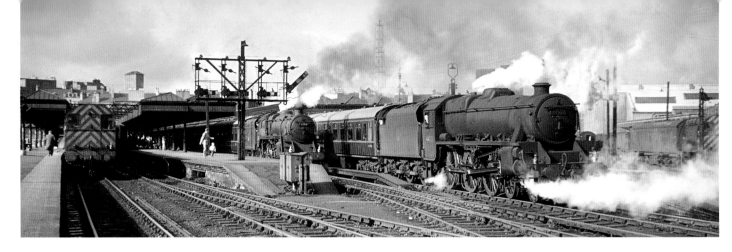

Journey's Beginning! A picture taken at Glasgow Buchanan Street on a bright 13th April 1963 showing Stanier Class 5MT No.44721, on the right, with the 10.15am train to Aberdeen, while BR Standard Class 5MT No.73106 awaits departure on the left with the 10.00am service to Inverness, which presumably it worked as far as Perth. Buchanan Street, perhaps the least impressive of Glasgow's terminal stations, was opened by the Caledonian Railway on 1st November 1849, replacing another station that was poorly sited in relation to the city centre. Construction of the line to Buchanan Street involved tunnelling beneath the Forth & Clyde canal, a legacy of this being a considerable initial climb, mostly at 1 in 79/98, as far as Robroyston. The premises were reconstructed by the London Midland & Scottish Railway in 1932 and a new glass-roofed concourse was installed, but the platform awnings were apparently obtained secondhand from the then recently-closed station at Ardrossan North. *Michael Allen*

The gradient out of Buchanan Street station was, as previously mentioned, quite taxing especially bearing in mind that it was not possible to gain any momentum before attacking the climb. In this picture Stanier Class 5MT No.45153 is depicted emitting a splendid smoke effect as it passes St Rollox motive power depot with the 10.15am Glasgow to Aberdeen train on 15th April 1963. Note the locomotive is carrying a snowplough: clearly the Scottish Region operating authorities did not leave anything to chance! Gresley A4 Class Pacific No.60027 *Merlin* is apparently being serviced at St Rollox shed, doubtless after arrival with an earlier working. No.60027 was transferred from Haymarket shed, Edinburgh, to St Rollox in May 1962 for use on the three-hour Glasgow to Aberdeen trains and remained there until it was moved to another Edinburgh shed, St Margarets, in September 1964. It survived in traffic for another year. *Michael Allen*

The first station of any importance after leaving Buchanan Street was Larbert – Cumbernauld had little more than a token service in the early 1960s – at which some Glasgow to Aberdeen trains called, but not the three-hour expresses. In this picture, taken on 20th July 1963, the 1.30pm Aberdeen to Glasgow train is seen departing behind nicely turned-out Class A2 Pacific No.60524 *Herringbone* which was based at Aberdeen (Ferryhill) shed at the time. This train was one of the slower services between the two cities and stopped at all but the smallest wayside stations: it had a journey time of exactly four hours. The arrival of this train at Glasgow coincided with the departure of the 5.30pm Aberdeen express and the memorable spectacle of A4-hauled trains arriving and departing at the same time could sometimes be observed. *Ken Falconer*

The 1.30pm Aberdeen to Glasgow train is seen again, this time at Bannockburn, south of Stirling, on 5th July 1965; motive power is provided by Gresley A4 Class Pacific No.60009 *Union of South Africa*. Despite being one of the slower services on the route this was a named train, the title 'The Grampian' being advertised in the public timetable. But the Scottish Region does not seem to have been too enthusiastic about the named trains on this line because headboards do not seem to have been carried nor individual services given any identity such as special carriage roof boards. Note the third vehicle in the formation: this is a miniature buffet car which was able to provide light refreshments. The section of line from Greenhill (near Larbert) to Perth was originally opened by the Scottish Central Railway in 1848. Note the colliery waste tip in the middle background, a reminder that coal mining was once a major industry in this area which brought a huge amount of business to the railway. *Roy Hobbs*

Scotland as many visitors will remember it, with a slate grey sky and rain that never seemed to stop. Here, the 7.10am Aberdeen to Glasgow train ('The Bon Accord') sets off in pouring rain on the final stage of its journey from Stirling to Glasgow behind Gresley A4 Class Pacific No.60007 *Sir Nigel Gresley* on 17th May 1965. The wagons with three vertical stripes on the left of the shot are vans equipped with shock absorbers for transporting delicate or easily damaged cargo and were known to railwaymen as 'Shocvans'. Part of Stirling locomotive shed can be seen on the right of the picture. In fairness to Scottish weather conditions, it has to be said that when the sun deigned to appear the lighting was almost always exceptionally bright and clear – ideal conditions for railway photography and, of course, the landscape was unrivalled. *Alan Chandler*

But it did not always rain at Stirling and this picture provides positive proof that it was possible on occasions to photograph steam trains in bright and sunny conditions, and what finer subject could there be than one of Sir William Stanier's magnificent 'Princess Coronation' Pacifics? Here, No.46250 *City of Lichfield* is depicted passing Stirling shed with the 3.15pm Aberdeen to London fish train on 3rd June 1963, a mundane duty for one of these thoroughbreds which were designed for working the heaviest West Coast main line expresses. By the date of this photograph, however, surviving members of this class were reduced to powering trains of this type following their displacement by diesels from more prestigious work. Part of Stirling shed can be seen on the left of the picture. The first shed was built on this site by the Scottish Central Railway in about 1850, the structure being enlarged in 1896. It was closed to steam traction on 13th June 1966. Note the North British Type 2 diesel locomotives on the extreme right, which had probably been dumped at the back of the shed while staff worked out how to fix them. These troublesome machines will go down in history as one of the most unsuccessful types introduced as part of the BR modernisation plan and must have cost the long-suffering taxpayer a fortune. *Roy Patterson*

GLASGOW (BUCHANAN STREET) TO ABERDEEN

A scene at the south end of Stirling station showing Stanier Class 5MT No.45360 awaiting departure with (what appears to be) a Dundee to Glasgow train. This station is an architectural gem and one of the most attractive and best-maintained in Scotland but the platform awnings, elegant though they are, do not give the impression of a really fine station. Part of the historic town, which is mostly on a much higher level than the railway station, can be seen on the left of the picture. This photograph was taken on 19th May 1964. *Martin Smith*

A grand total of 842 Stanier Class 5MTs (commonly known as 'Black Fives') was built, but only four examples, Nos.45154/6/7/8, carried names in the BR era. One engine, No.45155, was named *The Queen's Edinburgh* between 1942 and 1944. All four of these locomotives, which were named after Scottish regiments, were based at St Rollox shed in Glasgow for most of the 1950s, but Nos.45154 and 45156 were transferred to Newton Heath shed, Manchester, in April 1957. In this picture No.45158 *Glasgow Yeomanry* is seen taking water at Stirling on 15th August 1959 while powering the 4.15pm from Edinburgh (Princes Street) to Perth. This engine was built by Armstrong Whitworth & Co. in July 1935 and remained in traffic until July 1964. *Roy Patterson*

The exit from Stirling for northbound trains is on a slightly falling gradient so could not have been easier, but shortly before Bridge of Allan the foot of a six miles-long incline, mostly at 1 in 88/100, is reached and this lasts until the site of Kinbuck station. In this illustration an evening train from Glasgow to Dundee, headed by reasonably clean Stanier Class 5MT 4-6-0 No.44997, is seen at grips with the 1 in 100 gradient at the approach to Dunblane. The black smoke emitting from the Class Five's chimney no doubt pleased the photographer – could the fireman have timed it better? This picture was taken on a fine September evening in 1965. *Derek Penney*

The lovely stone bridge across Allan Water, the overhanging branches, the tower of Dunblane cathedral, not to mention the footpath which leads the eye down towards the railway. This spot has long been an irresistible photographic location for railway enthusiasts who no doubt also wished for an impressive smoke effect to add extra life to a picture. Unfortunately, on this occasion the photographer was probably disappointed but, even so, BR Standard Class 5MT No.73151, hauling an evening train to Dundee in September 1965, has produced an attractive picture. This machine was one of a batch equipped with Caprotti valve gear and these engines tended to be noisier than the conventional locomotives, so it is likely that the sound of No.73151 climbing away from Dunblane station was heard right across the town. *Colour-Rail*

What more could a railway photographer ask for? A sparkling clean locomotive, superb low evening lighting conditions, a uniform rake of maroon-liveried Mk 1 coaching stock and a memorable smoke effect. In this picture the 6.15pm Glasgow to Dundee train, hauled by Class A2 Pacific No.60530 *Sayajirao,* is seen running alongside the Allan Water, between Dunblane and Kinbuck on 30th August 1965. The gradient is 1 in 88 against northbound trains at this point, but this is unlikely to have troubled such a powerful locomotive pulling a modest six-coach load. The photographer appears to have been lucky with the sun on this occasion – note the large mass of grey cloud in the foreground. *Derek Penney*

GLASGOW (BUCHANAN STREET) TO ABERDEEN

The afternoon Aberdeen to London fish train, headed by BR Standard Class 6P5F Pacific No.72006 *Clan Mackenzie,* passes the site of Kinbuck station in June 1963. This was one of a large number of little-used wayside stations between Glasgow and Aberdeen that lost their passenger service from 11th June 1956, but when this picture was taken at least the platforms still appeared to be intact while the signal box, the roof of which is clearly visible above the train, was still very much in business. The enginemen on the footplate of No.72006 were doubtless taking things easy as their train drifted through the station on a falling gradient, but the crews of northbound trains no doubt breathed a huge sigh of relief when the former Kinbuck station hove into view as it marked the end of almost six miles of continuous climbing from just outside Stirling. *Colour-Rail*

GLASGOW (BUCHANAN STREET) TO ABERDEEN

The up afternoon travelling post office train from Aberdeen to Carstairs, which generally left Aberdeen at around 3.30pm, is depicted just south of Gleneagles on 20th May 1965. On arrival at Carstairs these vehicles were presumably attached to a similar working from Glasgow before continuing southwards to London. Motive power is provided by Stanier Class 5MT No.44724. This locomotive was constructed at Crewe in April 1949 and lasted in service until October 1966; it was one of a small series of ten of these machines built with a steel firebox. Just beyond this bridge the summit of a nine miles-long southbound climb from Forteviot was reached and the fireman was able to relax as his train sped downhill towards Stirling. *Alan Chandler*

Another shot just south of Gleneagles, looking down from the bridge seen in the previous picture, showing an altogether different scene. There is snow on the ground and the sun is shining – just the kind of conditions railway photographers dream about! The photographer's efforts have been spoiled to some degree, however, by the telegraph wires and, indeed, at this particular location there are poles on each side of the line, a railway photographer's worst nightmare! Here the 12.20pm Perth to London Euston train, which also conveyed through carriages from Aberdeen, is seen accelerating away from its Gleneagles station stop on 20th February 1964. The train included a restaurant car in its formation, which is probably just as well because passengers travelling to London were faced with a marathon 9½ hour journey, but at least they had the compensation of steam haulage over the first part of the run. Motive power is provided by reasonably clean BR Standard Class 6P5F Pacific No.72006 *Clan Mackenzie*. *Ken Falconer*

The 8.25am Glasgow to Aberdeen train, hauled by immaculate A4 Class Pacific No.60019 *Bittern,* has just topped the climb from Stirling and approaches Gleneagles station on a bright and sunny 28th May 1966. This train, and its corresponding 5.15pm return working, had seen a long spell of diesel haulage but, much to the delight and surprise of steam fans, A4 Class locomotives were again rostered for these trains from 18th April 1966. The 8.25am was officially titled *The Grampian. Roy Hobbs*

GLASGOW (BUCHANAN STREET) TO ABERDEEN

The 8.25am Glasgow to Aberdeen train is seen again, this time passing through Gleneagles station behind Gresley A4 Class Pacific No.60024 *Kingfisher*. This shot was taken on 29th June 1966. *Kingfisher* was based at Haymarket shed, Edinburgh, for many years for work on the crack East Coast Main Line expresses but after the A4s were ousted by diesels it was moved to St Margarets shed from where it was often employed on freight work to Tyne Yard, Newcastle, Aberdeen or up to Carlisle over the heavily-graded Waverley route, a line for which an A4 was hardly suited. Prior to its transfer to Aberdeen (Ferryhill) shed in May 1965 No.60024 received a 'light casual' repair at Darlington Works so should have been in reasonable fettle when it was put to work on the three-hour trains. *Michael Chown*

The branch line from Crieff Junction (later Gleneagles) to Crieff was promoted by the Crieff Junction Railway and received the Royal Assent on 15th August 1853. This company appears to have been a rather amateurish concern which, extremely optimistically, planned the opening for 1854 and apparently recruited staff before there was any work for them. The company even managed to upset the local laird by refusing his request for a private station and was consequently denied access to vital water supplies. There were also difficulties with the junction layout at Crieff Junction where the branch diverged from the Scottish Central Railway's Stirling to Perth route. Despite all of these problems the line eventually opened on 14th March 1856. An extension to Comrie was opened in 1893. 'Gleneagles for Auchterarder, Change for Crieff and Comrie' states the running-in board at the south end of Gleneagles station, which is surely one of the finest north of the border. Branch trains normally used the platform on the left. The premises date from 1919 when a splendid station was built to serve Gleneagles hotel, construction of which had commenced in 1913 but was halted by the outbreak of hostilities during the following year. Building resumed after the end of the First World War and the hotel opened on 5th June 1924. Ranked as one of the world's most luxurious, the Gleneagles hotel has variously been described as 'Scotland's gift to the world' and 'a truly great leisure palace'. This picture of Gleneagles station dates from 23rd August 1963 – note the carefully tended flower beds and exceptionally clean and tidy platforms. *Roy Denison*

An unidentified northbound working, in charge of Stanier Class 5MT No.44975, passes Hilton Junction signal box in May 1964. This train is something of a mystery because it appears to be a mixed train conveying freight stock in addition to passenger coaches. The line converging from the left is the former route to Cowdenbeath via Glenfarg which lost its passenger service from 5th January 1970. Trains between Edinburgh and Perth used to be routed this way but these now travel via Ladybank and Bridge of Earn along a stretch of line from which passenger services were originally withdrawn way back in September 1955. This route was reopened to passenger trains in October 1975, a rare case of a long-closed line being revived. Shortly after threading the junction, the train seen here would have plunged into Moncrieff tunnel, about 1½ miles south of Perth station.
Derek Penney

A southbound goods train, hauled by WD Class 2-8-0 No.90182 in typically grimy condition, approaches Moncrieff tunnel on 15th April 1963. This locomotive was allocated to Thornton Junction shed at the time of the photograph so it is likely that it would have taken the Cowdenbeath line at Hilton Junction: most of the train's consist is empty coal wagons presumably being returned to the Fife coalfield. The WD Class 2-8-0s were the unsung, unglamorous workhorses of heavy freight haulage of which a total of 935 were constructed, with 733 coming into BR ownership. The class was designed by R.A. Riddles for the Ministry of Supply during the Second World War and at the end of hostilities was employed on all BR regions, including the Southern Region for a time. This particular example, built by the North British Locomotive Co., began life as WD (War Department) No.7206 in August 1943 and entered BR service in December 1948. It was one of a small number of these engines based in Scotland and No.90182 was allocated to Thornton Junction shed as long ago as 1951, so it may have spent its entire BR working career in Scotland. *Michael Allen*

The southerly exit from Perth station provides a balanced and uncluttered photographic location as depicted here in this illustration of Stanier Class 5MT No.44979 accelerating away from its station stop with the 3.30pm Aberdeen to Glasgow Buchanan Street train on 15th August 1963. On this occasion this attractive location has been greatly enhanced by a superb cloud effect and lovely early evening lighting. Apart from an unidentified van on the rear, the train is formed entirely of LMSR-designed coaches. This working, which also conveyed through carriages to Edinburgh, was one of the slower trains on the Aberdeen to Glasgow route, taking 3 hours 42 minutes for the 153 miles-long journey. It was booked to spend thirteen minutes at Perth, presumably while the engine took water or an engine change took place. Perth motive power depot was located behind the photographer on the other side of the road bridge from where the picture was taken. *Colour-Rail*

A group of soberly dressed participants gather around 2P Class 0-4-4T No.55260 as it stands in the up platform at Coupar Angus station on 17th June 1962. This locomotive was based on McIntosh's 439 Class, a Caledonian Railway pre-grouping design that was perpetuated after the grouping took place in 1923. The engine was outshopped by Nasmyth Wilson & Co. in May 1925 and lasted until December 1962. The locomotive was working a short leg of a marathon ten-day tour of Scotland organised jointly by two societies and it is recorded that during that day the enthusiasts were treated to a ride along various obscure branch lines in the Forfar area that had long been closed to passenger operations, with 3F Class No.57581 as motive power. Among the lines visited were the Bridge of Dun to Brechin branch, the remaining stub of the Forfar to Brechin line as far as Careston, and the Alyth Junction to Newtyle goods line. The 0-4-4T took over after the train had returned to Alyth Junction and was *en route* to Perth. The two vintage vehicles immediately behind the engine are preserved Caledonian Railway coaches. Judging by this picture, the station appears to have been kept in a neat and tidy condition: note the colourful display of posters. *Colour-Rail*

Opposite: The twilight years of the A4 Class Pacifics. No.60024 *Kingfisher* simmers at the south end of Perth station as its water supply is replenished while working a Glasgow-bound train (probably the 1.30pm *ex*-Aberdeen) in September 1965. A strategically placed road bridge provided a wonderful grandstand from where to photograph steam engines as they took water. The Indian summer of the A4 Class Pacifics sparked enormous interest among the railway enthusiast fraternity and in this typical platform-end scene from that period a group of admirers cluster around the locomotive while an engineman chats to a member of the public. Two gentlemen are peering at *Kingfisher*'s tender – perhaps they have detected something amiss. Two sister engines were taken out of service in September 1965, Nos.60006 *Sir Ralph Wedgwood* and 60027 *Merlin*, while Nos.60031 *Golden Plover* and 60026 *Miles Beevor* succumbed in October and December respectively. This meant that only six of these locomotives remained active, all based at Aberdeen (Ferryhill) shed. The tracks curving away on the right lead to Dundee. *Colour-Rail*

The 6.20am Aberdeen to Perth 'local' stands at Forfar station's tightly-curving platform on 6th July 1966 with 'Black Five' No.44794 in charge. Ironically, the line between Kinnaber Junction and Perth was characterised by long, straight sections but Forfar station was located on a very sharp curve! The Strathmore route from Perth (Stanley Junction) to Forfar was opened by the Scottish Midland Junction Railway on 20th August 1848, while the line onwards to Kinnaber Junction was developed on a piecemeal basis over a number of years, the section from Forfar to Guthrie opening as early as 1st March 1839. It is recorded that the first through train from London to Aberdeen via Forfar passed through Strathmore on 1st April 1850. For many years Forfar was the principal traffic centre in the area from where various rural branches radiated and was a reasonably busy station. The first blow was struck on 4th August 1952 when the line to Bridge of Dun via Brechin and the Kirriemuir branch were axed on the same day. In early 1955 the line to Broughty Ferry was closed to passenger traffic while on 5th December of the same year the route to Arbroath suffered the same fate. So, in the space of just over three years Forfar lost all of its branch services. The end came for passenger trains along the Strathmore route on 4th September 1967 from which date Glasgow to Aberdeen trains were routed via Dundee, but Forfar retained a goods service from Perth until June 1982. Perhaps if the Strathmore line had directly served more of the larger towns in the area, such as Kirriemuir and Brechin, it may have survived. *Michael Chown*

GLASGOW (BUCHANAN STREET) TO ABERDEEN

A further view taken at Forfar. Pictured against the background of a deserted engine shed, which had been relegated to a sub-shed of Perth, former LMSR 4F Class 0-6-0 No.44257 undertakes a little light shunting on 23rd April 1962. The MR/LMSR Class 4F 0-6-0s were rare in Scotland with only 26 (of almost 600 engines) allocated there in July 1962; five were based at Perth, one at Fort William, and the rest were all in the Glasgow area.
Roy Hobbs

A picture taken at Bridge of Dun station on 19th July 1966, which seems to have been an absolutely glorious day. Here, a westbound train, probably the 1.30pm Aberdeen to Glasgow, hauled by Stanier Class 5MT No.44703, is seen moving off from its station stop. Bridge of Dun station lost much of its importance when the Brechin branch passenger trains were withdrawn and, in addition, it was located in a very thinly populated agricultural area, the nearest settlement of any consequence being Montrose, three miles distant, which was served by its own station on the East Coast Main Line. Consequently, few trains stopped there and in the summer 1963 timetable a mere four services in each direction were booked to call. Strange though it may seem, the line from Guthrie (on the Arbroath & Forfar Railway) to Bridge of Dun was opened by the Aberdeen Railway on 27th January 1848 with branches to Brechin and Montrose opening on the same day. Aberdeen was not yet connected to the main line system and passengers from the south had to resort to a horse-drawn coach. Aberdeen was eventually reached in stages, the last section from Portlethen opening in April 1850. *Charles Whetmath*

Apart from Gresley A4 Class Pacifics, and an assortment of other classes that passed through Bridge of Dun station on Glasgow to Aberdeen trains on a regular basis, another source of interest to observers were the activities of former North British Railway J37 Class locomotives. A small number of these sturdy engines survived at Dundee (Tay Bridge) shed until April 1967 for local freight work that included regular trips along the goods-only branch from Bridge of Dun to Brechin which, as previously mentioned, lost its passenger service in the early 1950s. Locomotives employed on this work were stabled at a small sub-shed at Montrose between duties. In this picture No.64620 is seen at Bridge of Dun station on 19th July 1966 whilst in the course of working to Brechin. *Charles Whetmath*

The 1.30pm Aberdeen to Glasgow Buchanan Street train is pictured at Drumlithie, with A4 Class Pacific No.60034 *Lord Faringdon* in charge, on 29th June 1966. By this date the number of A4s officially in traffic had dwindled to four, Nos.60004/19/24/34, but in reality the first-mentioned was already out of service, apparently being cannibalised to provide spares for No.60009 which had been sold for private preservation, so only three were available for use. No.60034 failed at St Rollox on 5th July and subsequently spent a period under repair in Eastfield repair shop, while the two other survivors were also out of action for most of that month. No.60019 spent much of July receiving attention at Ferryhill shed while No.60024 also failed and it, too, retired to Eastfield for repairs to be carried out. Large numbers of enthusiasts made the pilgrimage to Scotland to photograph and travel behind the A4s in their final weeks of service, but the majority must have been bitterly disappointed to find diesels working many of their turns while the three survivors languished out of use. At least some compensation was provided by the regular appearance of A2 Class Pacific No.60532 *Blue Peter* on the 1.30pm *ex*-Aberdeen and 11.02pm return. *Derek Penney*

Much to the delight and total surprise of steam fans the 8.25am Glasgow to Aberdeen and 5.15pm return train were, as previously stated, once again rostered for steam traction from 18th April 1966 after a long period of diesel haulage. The latter train is depicted near Carmont, about four miles south of Stonehaven, on a June evening in 1966 with No.60024 *Kingfisher,* in absolutely exemplary condition, at its head. The end of the A4s on this route was marked by a commemorative special on 2nd September hauled by *Bittern,* but against all the odds, No.60024 continued in action on freight work and had a final fling on the 5.15pm on 13th September after a diesel failure. It returned northwards the following morning on the 8.25am from Glasgow, thus ensuring that the class went out in a blaze of glory. The photographer comments that for most of the afternoon a sheet of cloud hung over the area which resulted in 'a sombre afternoon as chilly and cheerless as June could offer'. However, fortune favours the brave, or at least the persistent, and a chink in the clouds, that seemed to be confined to this location, appeared and lasted some considerable time while diesel-hauled trains sped southwards. By the time *Kingfisher* hove into view, however, the small patch of cloudless sky had grown considerably larger, no doubt to the photographer's intense relief, and this fine shot resulted, proving that on rare occasions luck can be on a railway photographer's side. *Derek Penney*

GLASGOW (BUCHANAN STREET) TO ABERDEEN

Most enthusiasts visiting Scotland during 1965/66 must have taken a dim view of the fact that three of the surviving A2 Class Pacifics, Nos.60528/30/32, were often to be seen standing idle at Dundee (Tay Bridge) shed on stand-by duties, main line work usually being confined to the odd freight turn to Edinburgh or Aberdeen. Surely they could have been put to better use on a Dundee to Glasgow express? During July 1966, however, there was a dire shortage of A4 Pacifics and No.60532 *Blue Peter* was loaned to Aberdeen (Ferryhill) to cover for the defective A4s, usually powering the 1.30pm Aberdeen to Glasgow and 11.02pm back, and proved to be a very capable performer. It is seen here near Fetteresso, just south of Stonehaven, on 1st September 1966. Presumably No.60532 had proved a welcome recruit at Ferryhill and the staff had decided to retain its services! *Derek Penney*

The exit from Aberdeen for southbound trains can be quite difficult especially when mist rolls in off the sea, making the rail surface slippery. The gradient is against up trains for the first seven miles and varies between 1 in 96 and 1 in 164, apart from one or two very brief, more moderate, sections. In this portrait, taken in 1962, Stanier Class 5MT No.44999 is seen tackling the climb away from the city with an unidentified southbound working. The North Sea forms the backdrop. No.44999 was one of 120 of these machines constructed at Horwich Works and this particular example emerged in March 1947. It remained in traffic until September 1966. *Colour-Rail*

Unfortunately, no pictures of trains at Aberdeen station were submitted for inclusion in this album, but here is a shot of the concourse at the station taken on 17th June 1962. Not surprisingly the concourse area was dominated by advertising hoardings extolling the supposed virtues of Tennent's lager, McEwan's Export and dancing at the Top Rank ballroom! The first station in Aberdeen opened at a somewhat remote site at Ferryhill on 1st April 1850, but four months later an extension to Guild Street, much nearer the city centre, was brought into use. A new, joint station was provided when the lines to the north and south of the city were connected in November 1867. The existing station was largely completed in 1914, the finishing touches being applied after the end of the First World War. *The late J.H.Moss / Stuart Ackley collection*

GLASGOW (BUCHANAN STREET) TO ABERDEEN

A dusting of snow on the ground, the sun shining out of a clear blue sky and a steam train! Could a railway photographer ask for more? This illustration depicts a Crieff to Gleneagles branch train, hauled by 'Black Five' No. 44980, ambling along at the approach to Gleneagles station on 20th February 1964. There was once a short goods-only branch which diverged from the Crieff line and served the Gleneagles hotel. When the hotel was being planned the designers apparently overlooked the need for a laundry with the result that one of the regular 'workings' over the hotel branch was that of a van full of laundry which ran on a daily basis to and from Edinburgh. *Ken Falconer*

Comrie station was looking rather neglected when this shot was taken on 23rd August 1963 and, indeed, the passenger service lasted less than a year after this scene was recorded, being withdrawn from 6th July 1964. The far platform certainly has a colourful display of lupins while roses adorn that nearer to the camera! Stanier Class 5MT 4-6-0 No.44979, deputising for a failed diesel railbus, which normally had sufficient capacity to cater for the small amount of traffic on offer, awaits departure for Gleneagles. The last train from here was worked by BR Standard Class 4MT 2-6-4T No.80093, reportedly laid on especially for a party of army cadets who were supposed to be travelling from Comrie to Gleneagles, but they failed to turn up! Missing the last train of the day is unfortunate, but missing the last train ever is surely unforgivable. *Roy Denison*

The 4³/₄ miles-long branch from Coupar Angus to Blairgowrie opened in 1855 and Blairgowrie was one of a number of hill-foot towns served by a branch off the main Perth to Aberdeen via Forfar line. Examination of the summer 1951 public timetable reveals an extremely sparse service consisting of a mere four trains in each direction on Mondays to Fridays to/from Coupar Angus with long gaps during the middle of the day. On Saturdays additional trains were advertised and these ran to/from Dundee via Newtyle, but no services operated on Sundays. A line with such a poor service was obviously a candidate for early closure and the passenger service was withdrawn from 10th January 1955, the same day that the Broughty Ferry to Forfar service was axed. The Blairgowrie branch retained goods facilities for almost a further eleven years, however, and this gave the opportunity for rail tours to visit this somewhat obscure line. Here, the rooftops of Blairgowrie form an attractive backdrop as former Caledonian Railway 4-4-0 Class 3P No.54465 awaits departure with the 'Scottish Rambler' rail tour on 23rd April 1962. Regrettably no examples of these lovely machines were saved for preservation – what an absolute tragedy! *Roy Hobbs*

The Brechin branch, opened on 1st February 1848, was originally part of a local line from Montrose via Dubton Junction and was one of the first lines in the area to be laid. In the 1951 summer timetable the advertised passenger service from Montrose to Brechin consisted of only a handful of trains each weekday, with no service at all on Sundays, and 1951 proved to be its last full year of operation, the service being withdrawn from 4th August 1952. Goods traffic to Brechin continued to be buoyant, however, because the rich soil in this area made it fertile farming country and much agricultural produce was carried, especially seed potatoes during the season. In the mid-1960s goods trains to and from Brechin were worked by veteran Class J37 0-6-0s based at Dundee (Tay Bridge) shed and sub-shedded at the small depot at Montrose. In this picture No.64577 is depicted heading away from Bridge of Dun towards Brechin with the daily goods working from Montrose in May 1966. *Roy Hobbs*

Despite closure to passengers fourteen years earlier the station building and much of the track layout at Brechin seem to be remarkably intact in this picture, which was also taken in May 1966. Miraculously, the attractive canopy at the front of the station also survived: perhaps it was a listed structure and thereby outside the remit of BR's demolition men. Here, the locomotive depicted in the previous shot is seen again, undertaking a little shunting after arrival from Montrose. Goods traffic continued here until 4th May 1981 and BR's decision to withdraw the service gave the green light to a local preservation society who took over the station building and site, and now operate to the former Bridge of Dun station on the erstwhile Forfar to Aberdeen line. *Roy Hobbs*

Powers were obtained in 1846 by the Stirling & Dunfermline Railway to construct a line from Thornton to Stirling, the line opening to Oakley in October 1849. Trains started running to Alloa on 28th August 1850 while Stirling was reached on 1st July 1852. There was a small engine shed at Alloa, which was a sub-shed of Dunfermline, and in this picture Class B1 4-6-0 No.61116 is seen passing in charge of a mixed goods train on 17th April 1965. Also visible, on the shed, is Class J38 0-6-0 No.65934 together with another, unidentified, locomotive of the same class. Note the member of BR staff striding energetically along the footpath. *Roy Hobbs*

The Ochil hills form the backdrop as Class WD 2-8-0 No.90515 ambles along near Bogside, on 6th July 1965, with a civil engineer's train of bogie bolster wagons conveying long-welded rails. No.90515 was originally built by Vulcan Foundry in January 1945 as War Department No.9251 and taken into BR stock in January 1948 and renumbered 63194. It was re-numbered 90515 in October 1949 and remained in BR service until withdrawn from traffic in February 1966. *Roy Hobbs*

Despite their dirty and dilapidated condition towards the end of the steam age, locomotive sheds always seemed to have an indefinable and totally irresistible appeal to railway aficionados. Perhaps it was the marvellous mix of various magical odours, such as smoke, steam, hot ash and oil that made these places so attractive to lovers of steam. Then there was the challenge, at least for unauthorised visitors, of walking around the shed without being forcibly ejected by the running foreman. Dunfermline shed, seen here, was certainly not one of the largest nor most famous sheds in Scotland, let alone in Great Britain, but even there when the sun was throwing shafts of light upon the rows of engines the atmosphere was something quite unique and not to be missed. Alas, this wonderful atmosphere has never been successfully recreated, at least in the author's view, in preservation. This picture, which shows Class WD 2-8-0 No.90386 on the right, was taken on 1st July 1966. *Michael Chown*

A short goods train, hauled by Class J38 0-6-0 No.65925, is seen at the approach to Thornton yard on 5th September 1966. Thirty-five of these powerful Gresley-designed 0-6-0s were built at Darlington works in 1926 to replace some of the assortment of ageing 0-6-0s inherited by the LNER in 1923. They spent their entire working lives in Scotland, mainly employed on hauling heavy coal trains in the Fife coalfield, and many were based at Thornton Junction or Dunfermline sheds. This particular engine was constructed in April 1926 and gave just over forty years' yeoman service before being withdrawn in November 1966. *Roger Merry-Price*

A view of Leslie viaduct with former NBR Class J37 0-6-0 No.64606 crossing with a train of empty coal wagons returning to Markinch on 28th June 1965. Opened in 1857, this little branch lost its passenger trains as long ago as 4th January 1932, but goods traffic survived, and in the 1960s the line gained a higher profile as a result of it being steam operated and possessing one of the finest photographic spots in Scotland, as seen here! Diesel shunters are reported to have taken over the duties after the elimination of steam traction in Scotland, but these did not see much use because the line was closed completely from 9th October 1967. *Colour-Rail*

The line between Perth and Dundee was opened in stages by the Dundee & Perth Railway, the section from Dundee westwards to Barnhill, just outside Perth on the east bank of the river Tay, opening on 24th May 1847. The remaining short stretch to Perth, which included the bridge across the river, was brought into use on 1st March 1849. The line is bordered by the southern slopes of the Sidlaw hills to the north and the river Tay to the south, this being in view for part of the way. The line is largely flat and does not have any engineering works of note, apart from the bridge across the river Tay. In this picture Class V2 No.60836 is seen leaving Dundee with a fully-fitted freight train for Perth in August 1966, part of the well-known Tay bridge just being visible on the right. In the mid-1960s Scotland was a happy hunting ground for steam enthusiasts because it became the last bastion of former LNER express passenger motive power. The final Class A2 Pacifics finished their days at Dundee (Tay Bridge) shed while the last A4s were based at Ferryhill shed (Aberdeen) for the expresses to Glasgow. The last surviving Class V2 2-6-2s were also allocated north of the border and No.60836 proved to be the *very last* representative of its class in service, not being withdrawn until the end of December 1966. *Colour-Rail*

In addition to being one of the last sheds with former LNER express passenger steam locomotives on its books, Dundee also maintained a fair number of Class J37 0-6-0s for local freight work. In this shot No.64577 scuttles through West Ferry station, east of Dundee, with the 1.30pm goods from Dundee to Montrose on 30th May 1966. The station here was closed from 4th September 1967. *Ken Falconer*

The Class J37s based at Dundee gained a certain amount of celebrity status as a result of their longevity and No.64547, seen here passing Broughty Ferry on a northbound freight on 20th July 1966, has evidently been the recipient of some unofficial embellishment. It might seem strange that these apparently unremarkable goods engines should be treated in this way, but by the date of this picture No.64547 was more than fifty years old, having been out-shopped from Glasgow's Cowlairs works in November 1915. Sadly, 1966 proved to be its last year in traffic but at least it had a very good innings, and it seems a shame that none of these unspectacular but workmanlike locomotives was saved from the cutter's torch. The last four survivors of this class were withdrawn in April 1967, just a few weeks before steam working officially ceased on the Scottish Region. The bridge in the background used to carry the former Caledonian Railway line from Broughty Ferry to Forfar, from which passenger trains were withdrawn on 10th January 1955. *Charles Whetmath*

The six miles-long line from Tillynaught to Banff was authorised on 27th July 1857 as part of the grandly-named Banff Portsoy & Strathisla Railway which ran from Grange, on the main Aberdeen to Inverness line, to Banff and Portsoy. The line to the latter location was later extended in stages to Elgin while that to Banff was generally worked as a branch from Tillynaught. In this picture nicely cleaned BR Standard Class 2MT 2-6-0 No.78054 is seen at Tillynaught with a two-coach train to Banff. In the summer 1963 timetable a service of ten trains in each direction was provided on weekdays only. The passenger service lasted until 6th July 1964 while freight traffic lingered until 6th May 1968. *Colour-Rail*

Waves crash against the rocks on the seashore as the 2.30pm Banff to Tillynaught train passes Golf Club House Halt on 18th July 1962. Motive power is provided once again by BR Standard 2-6-0 No.78054, emitting a magnificent smoke effect which no doubt pleased the photographer. The halt seen here opened in 1913 but in latter years no trains were booked to call, except on request to the guard or when there were passengers to take up. No.78054 was one of a small band of these locomotives based in Scotland and at the time of this picture it was allocated to Aberdeen (Ferryhill) shed. *Alan Chandler*

BANFF BRANCH

A picture of (what appears to be) a railway enthusiasts' special leaving Banff on 8th June 1957: once again the North Sea provides a distinctive backdrop. The station at Banff had a fine overall roof, no doubt to protect passengers from cold northerly winds. It is, perhaps, surprising that the Banff branch was never extended to reach the fishing town of Macduff less than a mile away on the opposite side of the Deveron estuary: instead the Great North of Scotland Railway (GNoSR) built a separate line from Inveramsay (near Inverurie) which must have been hopelessly uneconomic and closed to passengers as early as October 1951. The veteran locomotive powering the train is D40 Class 4-4-0 No.62277 *Gordon Highlander* which was built by the North British Locomotive Company and entered traffic in October 1920. It was based on a design originally introduced by the GNoSR in 1899 and is one of a later batch with detail differences. By the time this photograph was taken No.62277 had gained celebrity status as the last survivor of its class and was withdrawn from ordinary service exactly a year later. It was not broken-up, however, as it was scheduled for preservation by the British Transport Commission. The engine was restored as GNoSR No.49 *Gordon Highlander* and, much to the delight of many enthusiasts, was used on rail tours prior to being retired to the Glasgow Museum of Transport as a static exhibit. *Colour-Rail*

The small country junction of Craigellachie was where the Great North of Scotland Railway's Speyside line to Grantown-on-Spey and Aviemore diverged from the Keith to Elgin 'main' line. It was a 'V'-shaped layout with the Speyside line coming into the station on a tight curve. This view, however, shows the main-line part of the station, looking northwards in the direction of Elgin and Lossiemouth. Note the rather spindly footbridge linking the platforms, with its very informative signs advising passengers which platform to use, and the electric lighting of LNER vintage. Immediately beyond the road bridge the track became single and crossed the river Spey by means of a fine box-girder bridge which is partially visible. The passenger service between Boat of Garten and Craigellachie was withdrawn from 18th October 1965, while the last timetabled train of all to Craigellachie ran on 6th May 1968 when the service between Elgin and Keith via Dufftown was withdrawn. *The late J. Robertson / Stuart Ackley collection*

The tiny wayside station of Auchindachy was located about three miles south of Keith, and like many stations in this part of the world it served only a few nearby houses and little else. Perhaps most of its customers were fishermen spending a day on the river Isla which is just out of sight behind the road on the right of the picture. In this shot Class D40 4-4-0 No.62262 is seen passing through Auchindachy with a southbound goods on 2nd August 1954, so this is a really vintage illustration. The engine's front end has been spruced-up indicating that it had recently received some works attention, presumably at Inverurie. Built by Neilson Reid & Co. Ltd. in October 1899, No.62262 was withdrawn in October 1955 so it had a very long life. *Colour-Rail*

The unsurpassed scenic delights of the Inverness to Kyle of Lochalsh line, commonly known as the Kyle line, are legendary and include mountains, lochs and, where the line meets a sea loch, the odd fishing village. The route was pioneered by the Dingwall & Skye Railway with the aim of speeding up the movement of fish and livestock to the south and the company obtained its Act in 1865, opening to Strome Ferry on 19th August 1870. The company was beset by financial problems, however, and these caused it to seek parliamentary approval for a permanent terminus at Strome Ferry, thereby reducing the length of the railway from 63½ to 53 miles, but this caused difficulties with steamer connections due to the additional distance involved compared to Kyle. The Highland Railway took over the local company in 1877 and twenty years later, on 2nd November 1897, the long dreamed of extension to Kyle of Lochalsh became a reality. Some of the stations, such as Glencarron and Attadale, were built specifically to serve estates, but they eventually appeared in the public timetable for general use. The line includes some summits involving heavy gradients, notably those up to Ravens Rock and Luib (458 and 646 feet above sea level respectively). Another summit is Corriemuillie, west of Garve, which is 429 feet above sea level, and in this picture former Caledonian Railway 4-4-0 No.54487, piloting 'Black Five' No.44998, is seen battling up to the summit. They were photographed from the 10.30am Inverness to Kyle train on 2nd June 1960. *Roy Denison*

A further picture taken from the 10.30am *ex*-Inverness on 2nd June 1960. This shows a train from Kyle of Lochalsh coming into remote Achanalt station behind Stanier Class 5MT 4-6-0 No.44724 with the resident lady signalman exchanging the single line token with the fireman. This station is located in a very isolated location, with few buildings in the immediate area, and was doubtless provided with the requirements of the local landowner in mind. Note the lawn mower on the right. *Roy Denison*

From Strome Ferry to Kyle the railway follows the southern edge of Loch Carron and west of Plockton there is an almost unbroken series of cuttings and embankments as it threads the indented shoreline. Kyle of Lochalsh station was blasted out of solid rock when the line was built and in 1929, when a longer turntable was needed to accommodate larger locomotives, more clearance work was necessary. Here, 'Black Five' No.44998 is seen running round its train after arrival from Inverness, also on 2nd June 1960. One wonders what the barrels contained – whisky or beer? *Roy Denison*

Everybody's favourite view of Kyle of Lochalsh station and the dark, brooding mountains of the Isle of Skye across the water. The station building there is an island platform affair which is approached down a wide slope from the road, visible on the left of the picture. In the summer 1963 timetable three trains each way were advertised between Inverness and Kyle, one of which conveyed a buffet and an observation car. The working seen in this picture is a special which had been brought in by Stanier Class 5MT No.44978, seen here running round the stock presumably before being turned. The elegant pair of coaches at the far end of the formation are two preserved Caledonian Railway vehicles that were a familiar sight on rail tours in Scotland in the 1960s. Perhaps the most striking thing about this picture is the congested nature of the sidings that appear to be full of goods wagons of a variety of types, ranging from cattle vans to oil tank wagons. What happened to all of that railborne traffic? *Colour-Rail*

The running-in board on the left clearly indicates the location of this photograph, which was taken on 4th June 1960. The station here took its name from Thomas Telford's embankment of 1817 which crosses over the river Fleet at this point and saves a considerable detour: today it carries the A9 main road. A barrow-load of parcels has been unloaded from the brake van, a Stanier Class 5MT 4-6-0 'blows off' impatiently at the far end of the platform but the starting signal stubbornly remains at danger. Meanwhile a gentleman sits on the platform seat reading, apparently oblivious to everything around him. The Mound was the junction for the branch to Dornoch, the branch platform being at a slightly lower level on the left of the shot. The station was located in a very isolated position, its only purpose being for interchange purposes, and it was closed when the Dornoch line was axed from 13th June 1960. *Roy Denison*

The 161½ miles-long line from Inverness to Wick was constructed over a fourteen year period. Work began on the Inverness & Ross-shire Railway in 1860 but progress was slow and the line was opened in stages, the first being from Inverness to Dingwall, opened on 11th June 1862. It was 1874 before the first train arrived at Wick. The final section of line opened was that from Helmsdale to Wick and in this picture, taken on 3rd June 1960, former Caledonian Railway Class 3P 4-4-0 No.54495 sits in the up platform at Helmsdale while a Wick-bound train, headed by an unidentified Stanier Class 5MT is in the down platform. Catering facilities were provided on certain services between Inverness and Helmsdale, while on others the restaurant car worked to and from The Mound. Between Golspie and Helmsdale the line runs close to the sea, but when it reaches the latter point it turns inland and runs in a northerly direction following the river Helmsdale. Note the collection of grounded van bodies and other elderly items of rolling stock in the goods yard. *Roy Denison*

A scene at Georgemas Junction station, taken on 4th June 1960, showing Stanier Class 3MT 2-6-2T No.40150 simmering in the Thurso branch platform. The branch curves to the right behind the footbridge. This is the most northerly junction station in Great Britain, but it is located in a very thinly populated area and is unlikely to attract much originating traffic. The nearest settlement of any size is the small village of Halkirk. The name 'Georgemas Junction' came from a local fair which took place on St George's Day at nearby Sordale Hill. No.40150 was the regular Thurso branch engine for some years and was based at Wick shed for that purpose. It was one of 139 locomotives of this type built during the Stanier era and was that designer's version of the Fowler Class 3MT 2-6-2Ts. No.40150 was constructed at Derby Works in September 1937 and survived until December 1962. The signal box, just visible in the background, dated from 1894 when the line north of Invergordon was resignalled by Dutton & Co. The box was closed in 1985. *Roy Denison*

The 8.40am train to Inverness waits to leave Thurso station on 4th June 1960. Motive power is provided by Stanier Class 3MT 2-6-2T No.40150. Two pigeon vans sit in the adjacent platform and the large piles of opened pigeon baskets on the platform indicate that the birds have been released. Like most stations in this area Thurso, constructed using local stone, was functional rather than ornate, its most prominent feature being the small train shed, the roof of which was supported by wooden trusses. Part of the modestly-sized goods yard is visible on the right. *Roy Denison*

Former Caledonian Railway 4-4-0 No.54495, which has been polished to perfection, sits out in the sunshine at Wick engine shed on 6th September 1961. This locomotive was designed by Pickersgill as Class 72 and built by Armstrong Whitworth in June 1921. It was withdrawn by BR in February 1962. The locomotive shed here had two roads and was closed in 1962. The line north of Helmsdale was promoted by the Sutherland & Caithness Railway which obtained an Act of Parliament on 13th July 1871. The route crossed some wild and very inhospitable terrain and was opened to traffic on 28th July 1874. *John Langford*

In the 1890s the Highland Railway put forward a plethora of proposals for light railways under legislation that encouraged their development. These included highly optimistic plans to build light railways in very sparsely populated parts of the Highlands and among the schemes suggested were lines from Achnasheen to Aultbea, Culrain to Lochiver and Lairg to Laxford. The branch from The Mound to Dornoch was one of only two proposed schemes to come to fruition (the other being the line from Wick to Lybster), and the 7³/₄ miles-long Dornoch Light Railway (DLR) was authorised in August 1896 and opened on 2nd June 1902. The Mound took its name from Telford's embankment across the waters of Loch Fleet which was laid in 1817. The DLR owned a hotel at Dornoch which catered for visitors to Scotland's smallest cathedral city and this establishment survived to become a British Transport hotel under the BR regime. In more prosperous times three trains were timetabled each weekday, but in BR days only two were scheduled in each direction, all running as mixed trains. Motive power was provided for many years by two former Highland Railway 0-4-4Ts, Nos. 55051 and 55053, dating from 1905, and when these were finally pensioned off in the late-1950s BR surprisingly drafted in two Western Region pannier tank locomotives, Nos. 1646 and 1649. The latter is seen at The Mound in the Dornoch branch platform on 10th September 1958. The main Inverness to Wick line is obscured by the fence on the right of the shot. *Gerald Daniels*

DORNOCH BRANCH

There were three intermediate stations on the line, Cambusavie Platform, Skelbo and Embo. The wild and windswept nature of the landscape in this beautiful part of the world can be seen in this picture of No.1649 leaving Embo with a mixed train for Dornoch on the same day as the previous photograph. Prior to moving to Scotland to take up its new role No.1649 was based at St Philip's Marsh shed in Bristol – quite a change of scene!
Gerald Daniels

A small crowd of passengers gathers on the platform at Dornoch station prior to the departure of the 1.00pm train to The Mound, on 3rd June 1960. No.1646 raises steam on the right of the shot, while the unpretentious station building is on the left. The background is dominated by the considerable mass of Dornoch cathedral. The railway line from Inverness to Wick is extremely circuitous, mainly due to the fact that it has to wend its way around both the Cromarty and Dornoch firths, the distance by rail from Inverness to Dornoch being 88 miles as opposed to the straight line distance of 29 miles. *Roy Denison*

The driver of 1600 Class 0-6-0PT No.1646 awaits the 'right away' from the guard prior to departure with the 1.00pm train from Dornoch to The Mound, also on 3rd June 1960. This engine was the first of the two panniers to be introduced on the line, arriving in 1957, with No.1649 following during 1958. The line was closed completely by BR on 13th June 1960 but the ScR obviously took a liking to the pannier tank locomotives, finding them alternative employment as station pilots at Dingwall. This mundane work, which apparently included heating a Post Office vehicle, continued well into 1962 and reportedly became the last booked steam turn on the Highland section. *Roy Denison*